Sunbirds in the Morning, Grey Hornbills at Dusk

Also by Bulbul Sharma

My Sainted Aunts

The Perfect Woman

Anger of Aubergines

Banana Flower Dreams

Shaya Tales

Devi

Eating Women, Telling Tales

Now that I am Fifty

Tailor of Giripul

Murder in Shimla

CHILDREN'S BOOKS

Fabled Book of Gods and Demons

The Children's Ramayana

The Book of Indian Birds

Birds in My Garden and Beyond

Sunbirds in the Morning, Grey Hornbills at Dusk

Nature Rambles Through Delhi

BULBUL SHARMA

SPEAKING TIGER

SPEAKING TIGER BOOKS LLP
125A, Ground Floor, Shahpur Jat,
Near Asiad Village, New Delhi - 110 049

First published by Aleph Book Company 2014
This edition published by Speaking Tiger Books 2023

ISBN: 978-93-5447-601-3
eISBN: 978-93-5447-603-7

10 9 8 7 6 5 4 3 2 1

Printed at Chaman Enterprises, New Delhi

For my beloved family who have never shown any interest ever in nature, yet have listened to my tales. And for my bird-watching friends.

CONTENTS

INTRODUCTION

Grey wings flapping quietly, a ripe red berry in his beak, the male Grey Hornbill flies home at dusk unheeding of the rush hour traffic. Horns blare, fumes rise but the Hornbill ignores it all. His only concern is to get back to his wife safely and give her this choice morsel of food.

Delhi is the only capital city in the world where, right in the middle of a traffic jam, you can see a handsome Grey Hornbill or a Golden-backed Woodpecker searching for dinner. Oblivious to noise, traffic or crowds the birds carry on with their endless chores of feeding, nesting, and wooing their mates. The capital city, with its gardens and parks, scrub forests, and avenues of old trees, has an amazing range of different habitats where you can see as many as a hundred species of birds with hardly any effort. Over the years I have seen Scarlet Minivets dancing in Lodhi gardens, Baya weavers frantically building nests in an old garden, Munias gossiping amongst the scrub hedges along the Ring Road. While in most other countries you have to really struggle to spot birds, in Delhi they come right up to you, watch you with trusting eyes and then move on to the task at hand.

Each species likes to hang out with its own kind like us humans and you will rarely find a woodland bird flying into a scrub forest area unless something very exciting to eat is on offer like a Jamun tree laden with ripe fruit or a field of wild grass with seeds.

New Delhi with its vast open parks, avenues of old trees and green roundabouts; Old Delhi with secret groves of ancient trees and hidden corners of green; the riverine habitat of the Jamuna; and rocky scrub forests on the outskirts of Delhi often dotted with cultivated fields–each area is host to many fascinating creatures.

An hour's drive will take you to the huge Sultanpur lake where you can see migratory birds basking in the winter sunshine and if you still want more, then the famous Bharatpur lakes with their abundant birdlife are not too far.

Delhi is a birdwatcher's city with at least twenty birds on display at any given time. You will see bulbuls, mynas, woodpeckers and bee-eaters in almost every park or garden. In other cities, I find, there are a dozen birdwatchers, armed with heavy cameras and high tech binoculars, watching one poor little bird. I feel sorry for the creature who is trying its best to find a safe place to hide out of sheer fright. But in Delhi, go to any park or garden and you will meet a bird at once and then a few more as you walk ahead. I have been fortunate enough to live here all my life and seen most of its resident birds along with many migratory visitors.

I can bore people endlessly about how I used to birdwatch where the bustling Saket malls are now and how I knew a man who fished in a pond where the sprawling Vasant Kunj colony stands like a citadel of concrete. A small, blue Common Kingfisher lived in this pond and we used to see its turquoise wings flash as we walked through the fields. These jewel-like kingfishers are not so common now and the one you see everywhere is its bigger relative, the White-breasted Kingfisher. Unlike the smaller bird which likes to stay near water bodies, this one is equally happy in dry areas and eats almost anything its greedy eyes can spot.

In the Seventies, I could walk from my house in Haus Khas across mustard fields to the lonely, quiet village of Haus Khas. No one had heard the word 'trendy' then, in this sleepy, hookah-smoking village where buffaloes had the right of way. Hundreds of Rose-ringed Parakeets flew in at dusk changing the colour of the sky from grey to green for a few moments. There were mongoose colonies under the ruined walls of monuments and there must have been a large population of snakes and rodents because every mongoose I met on my rambles looked smug and well-fed.

Gradually the city changed and as I grew older, it grew with me but in the reverse order. It is now younger, faster, noisier, and full of new things while I have grown older and, like many other people of my generation, a bit weary and suspicious of all the bewildering and new aspects of the city.

Fortunately one thing remains unchanged—Nature rambles on happily in Delhi.

The Coppersmiths are still there in Lodhi Garden, chanting their monotonous song, and the Spotted Owlets lurk on old keekar trees on the ridge, staring at the world with surprise. You may be lucky enough to see a deer in the scrub forests on the outskirts of Delhi and maybe an Indian hare too. Mongoose lurk in the old gardens of New Delhi, along with Crow Pheasants, birds with a guilty secret, and an occasional langur may drop by to inspect the trees.

The handsome, black-faced langur (*Presbytis entellus*) is not as aggressive and ill-mannered as its cousin the Rhesus Macaque—our familiar 'bandar' so loved by Kipling. In fact many of these langurs are 'salaried employees' of the Government of India and work more diligently than their human counterparts, arriving every day at nine and working till five in various government offices and hospitals! I met one such hardworking langur babu in AIIMS where he was busy chasing the other monkeys, the Rhesus Macaque away. At first they just glared at each other and then suddenly there was an explosion of rude words and much snarling and baring of teeth. The 'bandar' had many nasty things to say but our official langur held his territory with dignity and the Rhesus gang scampered away muttering rudely. 'The problem is that the langur goes off duty sharp at five and then the other monkeys attack,' complained one nurse, protecting her bag from an angry monkey glaring down from the roof, obviously waiting to seek revenge sharp at five o' clock.

Delhi's flowering trees will always have something for the monkeys to eat but they seem to prefer alu parathas to the green mangoes that summer offers or sweet, purple jamuns that the rains bring. They have grown fat and lazy and seem to have forgotten those tough days when they had to forage for food in the scrub forests of Delhi under constant threat from leopards and tigers. Yes, once upon a time Delhi had tigers, leopards, jackals, hyenas, and pythons residing in their chosen habitats. The vast dry scrub forest land, the rocky wilderness, and the acres of swamps by the river Jamuna gave them a safe home. There are accounts of Mughal princes hunting them and later of how the British tried their best to grab at least one tiger trophy to boast about back home. Now there are bustling colonies and high rise buildings where these wild animals once roamed and the only mammals you will see easily are the mongooses and the monkeys. I have sometimes heard a few jackals howling in the Ridge area. I think they are trying to tell us that this city was once theirs.

Every season brings a new flavour to Delhi's parks and gardens and even the smallest garden will change its colours to suit the mood. Sometime you may not recognize a tree as it changes its foliage from summer to winter. The laburnum, for instance, looks like a shabby, bad-tempered tree in winter when it has no flowers. Its branches are covered with long, brown sticks which rattle in the breeze like witches muttering curses. Then as spring leaves, making way for summer, the blossoms arrive slowly, and then one day the tree suddenly becomes this fairy tale creature with streaming golden flowers, a magical yellow pyramid, shimmering in the sunlight.

The cycle of seasons, each one with its own particular

trees, flowers, food, and clothing is what I love about Delhi. The summer heat with its blinding sunlight that brings out the brightest Gulmohur blossoms, the rainy season that makes the peacocks dance in the parks, the bitterly cold, grey winter days when roasted peanuts taste the best and our brief, fleeting spring with its festival of 'English' flowers.

Delhi wears a verdant, green cloak during the rains, changes it for a thick woollen shawl for winter and then quickly discards it to make us sweat in the summer. We, who have always lived in Delhi, follow the rules and change our daily lives according to the seasons. If you spend a year in Delhi, you will realize why the residents of Delhi are so tough and a bit thick-skinned.

Unlike Mumbai with its soothing sea breeze, hot and humid Kolkata with deliciously cool evenings, and forever tranquil Goa and Bengaluru, Delhi makes its residents struggle for a bit of warmth in winter and for a spot of cool shade in summer.

There are plenty of rewards like the glorious summer flowering trees, the crisp cold air of a winter's morning, the scented nights of the rainy seasons. We love to complain as we shiver in the biting cold, burn under the harsh summer sun, get flooded during the monsoon. But then there is the beautiful Delhi spring that brings out a host of fragrant flowers and the gentle sunshine brings joy to our hearts.

January is a quiet month with mist and fog hiding the sun. It rises quietly, a pale reddish gold sphere, and makes a brave attempt to shine on the trees but soon a cruel grey curtain crawls out of nowhere to cover it and we are back to shivering and shaking like people in a Charles Dickens' novel. You wonder if this is the same city where hot, dusty winds will blow in four months' time, and the same weak and pale sun will burn ferociously on every blade of grass.

Delhi is famed for its extreme climate and most of its residents suffer the intense cold and cruel heat with an equal amount of grumbling. The trees are not very happy as the new year dawns since they have not seen sunlight for the past few days. But the birds cannot stop singing all day long, they like the cold weather since there is plenty to eat and they can build up their strength for the nest-building days to come. The Tailor Bird calls out in a high-pitched tone as it flits about restlessly searching for something to eat. For a bird that is so tiny, it has a really loud call and you will hear it long before you can spot its green feathers in the foliage. The Tailor Bird was made famous by Kipling in his children's stories as 'Darzi' since it stitches up leaves with its sharp, pointed beak to make a nest. It is almost impossible to find its leafy home even if you are standing right next to it. Our clever 'darzi' always chooses two or three pliant leaves and makes a little cone by stitching them up with thin yarn or grass and then places a soft, feathery, woolly nest in the centre. But since it cannot stop boasting about how clever it is—a bit like a fashion designer, you can sometimes find the nest by listening carefully and then following its incessant chatter.

The Purple Sunbird is cheerful because there are plenty of tiny insects to eat and the garden now has a rich selection of winter flowers full of nectar. The male is singing because he is happily anticipating the new glossy, metallic-purple plumage he will acquire for the breeding season. The female, a greenish brown bird, watches him with quiet disapproval as she looks for food. The Sunbird has a long pointed beak that it dips into flowers to sip nectar and help in cross pollination. You will see it emerge, its glossy head covered with yellow pollen dust and this will get transferred when it flies off to explore another flower, usually of the same variety.

From end of November till mid February is a good time to head out to the open fields outside Delhi and then beyond to Sultanpur Lake where the migratory birds are wintering. Most of them have flown a long distance from their breeding grounds in Central Asia, braving hostile lands, freezing temperatures, and icy storms. They start arriving in Sultanpur by November and are well settled to celebrate the new year with us.

Getting up at dawn on a dark and cold January morning is not an easy thing to do unless you are really keen on birds. I have sometimes bulldozed my family into coming with me and when we do arrive at sunrise to witness a spectacular sight of hundreds of migratory geese and ducks, they are yawning and sullen with sleep. Now only a mention of hot chai and samosas will wake them up; a bribe, of course, but for a good cause.

The Pintail Ducks, though, elegant brown and black with pointed tails, are alert even at dawn. Every year they are usually the biggest group on the lake. You will see them either upending in the water or floating about in small groups, looking like a bunch of smart, eager-to-achieve-everything, corporate guys gathering for an AGM. You will find them constantly shifting and twisting their pointed tails, restlessly looking around to make sure the other birds have not grabbed something better and bigger. Next to them are the slow and steady Greylag Geese. Though these two big migratory groups may hang out together they are very different from each other. The geese move slowly and gracefully like dignified old ladies, their pink bills gleaming in the gentle winter sunlight. The only thing that makes them move faster is the sight of a Marsh Harrier hovering above their heads. Then with a splash and a flutter of a hundred wings the birds rise and flee, only to settle down a few minutes later with much grumbling and honking.

The Marsh Harrier, despite its nasty ways, is a bird I like to watch for hours. It loves to rise high in the air with its wings stretched out and then suddenly it will swoop to grab a helpless duck. It has a gleaming, pale brown head that catches the light as the bird twists and turns in the air. Sometimes it will chase the geese and ducks just for fun, making them honk hysterically as they rush from one end of the lake to the other. At first you will hear a low, long drum beat as the geese take off and then a loud honking will echo all over the lake as the entire flock rises in the air, abusing the Marsh Harrier.

There are smaller groups of other duck species floating about on the lake and it takes me a long time to identify them through the mist. The Mallard is easy because of his green head and yellow beak. But watch out, there is another green-headed duck relaxing next to him and this one is called the Shoveller because of its flat shovel-like bill. A quick flash of a russet head tells you that the Red-crested Pochard is also in the crowd and its darker headed cousin, the Tufted Pochard, is lurking here too, its tiny yellow eyes gleaming in the faint light. The handsome reddish gold Brahminy Duck, which comes to winter in Delhi from Ladakh and Tibet, is a favourite of miniature painters but not that easily seen now. The Common Teal, Gadwall, and Wigeon have also flown in from their breeding grounds in Central Asia, Siberia, and northern Europe. There used to be another duck gliding amongst them, its beautiful bright pink head an envy of all other birds, but, alas, the Pink-headed Duck was last seen in 1935 and is considered extinct now.

Ornithologists are not really sure how these birds find their way, year after year, to their winter feeding grounds. There are various theories and one of them is that they use the sun to plan their routes. The migrating birds maintain their course from the angle the sun makes with the earth at the appropriate season and at night they are guided by major constellations of stars.

What is amazing is that even young birds with no previous experience of destination or route, manage to fly thousands of miles to their winter grounds. Many of these migrating ducks and geese fly over the Himalayas at heights of 3,000 to 5,000 metres to shorten their journey.

The winter sun warming their backs, the abundant

vegetarian and fishy food to eat and company of other migratory birds obviously makes their long and arduous journey worthwhile. Our resident Spotbill duck with bright yellow spots on its beak and flashy orange legs is happy to share the lake with these visitors and never chases them away.

The Nilgai in the shade of the keekar tree watches us suspiciously and then scampers off clumsily into the bushes. There are flamingoes here too, gliding in the mist like elegant ballerinas, always moving in graceful co-ordination. Their specialized beaks have to be used with skill and that is why they curve their long necks so that the bill is upside down and can sift food from the shallow water by moving from side to side. Not an easy task but they seem to do it effortlessly and with grace.

Behind them you may see a group of stout pelicans floating about slowly and aimlessly like toy sailboats. Their large beaks are very good for catching fish though I have never seen one actually getting one. All they seem to do is swim from one end of the lake to the other, pause and then head back. Sometimes you can see pelicans in the Delhi Zoo but their feathers always look dull unlike the ones in Sultanpur. Must be the boredom of being in a zoo with nothing to look at except rowdy crowds of humans.

The trees around the lake are full of birdlife too but you have to be careful not to fall into the squelchy mud like I did, trying to get a closer look. As I crashed through the reeds, startling a Purple Moorhen about to sit down for its breakfast, an angry young Nilgai rose from the island and headed straight for me. I froze with terror, counting my last few moments, but, fortunately, the Nilgai got distracted by a sweet young female Nilgai, just before it reached me. The pair stared at each other for a while and then as I rose from the muddy waters, they walked into the sunrise. It took a week for me to scrape the fishy smelling clay off my shoes and even after that dogs would sniff suspiciously and growl at my feet whenever I wore those unfortunate shoes.

From a very young age, I have waded through muddy pools in search of birds. I grew up in Bhilai, then a small town in Madhya Pradesh, it was safe to let children wander around in the vast open countryside. I remember the mango orchards, the ponds, and the thorny scrub forests vividly till this day. It is part of my DNA, I think.

Every winter I wait eagerly to see a small bird—the Blue Throat. This tiny bird wears a smart blue scarf around its little neck and hops about looking for insects under the leaves. It is a friendly bird but because of its tiny size it is not very easy to spot. But if you see a pile of dry leaves shaking, then wait and watch. The Blue Throat may emerge to greet you with its merry, sparkling eyes. Once a bird came up really close to us and ate a bit of the tomato sandwich we offered it. It stayed with us for a while, cocking its little head as if it wanted to make polite conversation with us or thank us for the tidbit. Then it flew away to search for insects under the tree having had enough of vegetarian fare, I suppose. Its trusting habits worry me and I hope it will have a safe journey home to its breeding grounds in the Himalayas.

WINTER

The skies have turned grey and cold
as the sunlight fades at noon
Now the trees stand forlorn
The birds fall silent
O mighty Sun God
Send us your arrows of golden fire
To protect us from winter's wrath
To shield us in a circle of warmth.

~ ANONYMOUS

January in Delhi, as in the rest of north India, is a bitterly cold month with mist and fog hiding the sun. Every morning, the sun rises quietly, a pale reddish-gold sphere, and tries to make a brave attempt to shine but soon a cruel grey curtain crawls out of nowhere to cover it and we are back to shivering as we huddle around electric or wood fires. The streets turn quiet as soon as the sun makes a hasty retreat after a failed attempt to brighten the day, and a cold, silent dusk falls all over the city. It seems as if a huge net of frozen mist has been sent down from the skies to cover its trees, gardens and homes. You wonder if this is the same city where hot dusty winds will blow in four months' time and the same weak and pale sun will blaze ferociously on every blade of grass and turn them white.

The trees are not very happy as the new year dawns since they have not seen sunlight for the past few days. But the birds, always looking on the brighter side of things, cannot stop singing. They like the cold weather since there is plenty to eat and they can build up their strength for the nest-building days to come. The tailorbird calls out in a high-pitched tone as it flits about restlessly, searching for something to eat. For a bird which is so tiny, it has a really loud call and you will hear it long before you can spot its green feathers amongst the foliage. Most people do not believe it is this tiny green bird with a long tail which is making this loud noise and keep looking for a bigger bird.

The tailorbird was made famous by Kipling in his stories as Darzi, and to live up to its name, it stitches up leaves with its sharp pointed beak to make a nest. It is almost impossible to find its leafy home even if you are standing right next to it. Our clever darzi chooses two or three pliant leaves and makes a little cone by stitching them up with thin yarn or grass and then places a soft feathery woolly nest in the centre. But since he cannot stop boasting about how clever he is—a bit like a fashion designer—you can sometimes find the nest by listening carefully to its incessant chatter and following the sound.

A tailorbird built a nest in a flower-pot in my veranda last year and I thought it was very silly of the bird to place its nest in such an unsafe position. I could not help it since the leaves had been stitched so carefully and two tiny eggs had already been laid by the mother bird.

People passed by the nest all day, we sat and talked right above it, the floor under the nest was swept and the flower-pot watered. Nothing damaged the nest, and one day two little fledglings hopped out. They quickly learnt to fly under their parents' careful supervision and then the entire family flew away. Before they left the mother bird gave me a sharp look which said, 'See, I am not as stupid as you thought.'

With the garden now ready with a rich selection of

winter flowers full of nectar, the Purple Sunbird is cheerful as there are plenty of tiny insects to eat. A sudden flash of olive green and purple means the Purple Sunbird is here. The male is singing because he is happily anticipating the new glossy, metallic-purple plumage he will acquire for the breeding season. The female, a greenish-brown bird, watches him with quiet disapproval as she looks for food. I have a feeling she thinks the male spends too much time preening his feathers and she has to do all the hard work. Both have long pointed beaks which they dip into flowers to sip the nectar and help in cross pollination.

The female will start her nest-building activities soon and the male, afraid to get his glossy new feathers dirty, does nothing to help her. She tirelessly collects bits of grass, fine twigs and dried leaves to construct an intricate nest which has a tiny porch above the entrance to keep out the rain. Once she has finished building the nest, she very cleverly camouflages it with cobwebs, bits of bark and caterpillar droppings. One may well be fooled into thinking, on seeing this nest, that it is a clump of rubbish hanging on the branch, blown in by the wind. I once sat all morning under a sunbird's nest which had been built on a low branch and never realized it was its official residence till it flew out suddenly. The bird must have been waiting for an hour for me to leave and then finally got fed up and flew away, just the way we often try to dodge unwelcome guests who had overstayed their welcome.

The male sunbird does help to feed the fledglings but

still takes time out to polish his beautiful breeding plumage which will soon disappear after which he will become a plain bird again. However, if you look closely, you will see a faint streak of purple to remind you of its former good looks.

Despite the bitterly cold and foggy mornings, this is a good month to head out to the open fields outside Delhi and then beyond to the vast Sultanpur lake where flocks of migratory birds are wintering. Most of them have flown a long distance from their breeding grounds in Central Asia, Tibet and Ladakh, braving hostile humans, freezing temperatures and icy storms. They start arriving in Sultanpur by September and are well settled to celebrate the new year with us.

Getting up at dawn on a January morning is not an easy thing to do unless you are really keen on birds. I often have to bribe my family to come with me and when we do arrive at sunrise to witness a spectacular sight of hundreds of migratory geese and ducks, they are yawning and sullen with sleep. Now only a mention of hot chai and samosas will wake them up. Once I took a group of friends to Sultanpur and they complained that the ducks and geese were so drab and dull.

'We thought you would show us something spectacular like a peacock or a cockatoo,' they whined as I pointed out a huge flock of Bar-headed Geese freshly arrived from Central Asia.

'What about a tiger? Maybe a small leopard?' asked a sleepy friend.

If they only realized how difficult it is for these birds to reach Sultanpur and other lakes they would admire the birds' courage and determination to survive. What is amazing is that even young birds with no previous knowledge of their destination or the route manage to fly thousands of miles to their winter grounds. Many of these migrating ducks and geese fly over the Himalayas at heights of 3,000 to 5,000 metres to shorten their journey. Ornithologists are not really sure how these birds find their way year after year to their winter feeding grounds. There are various theories and one of them is that they use the sun to plan their routes. The migrating birds maintain their course from the angle the sun makes with the earth at the appropriate season and at night they are guided by major constellations.

The migration route is a long and dangerous one but the birds know they have to leave Central Asia where winter conditions are very severe and there is no food supply. They figured out, probably thousands and thousands of years ago, that they could get plenty of good food and sunshine if they flew down to India. They had worked out the magical escape-to-seek-the-sun idea long before package tourism was thought of.

So every year, wave after wave of ducks and geese fly thousands of miles over the snow-capped Himalayas and frozen lakes to reach their winter feeding grounds. From September to March they bask in the sunshine, they eat as much as they can and grow plump happily and with no guilt. This layer of fat they acquire during their winter holidays in

India will help them survive the long journey home. So the fatter they are, the better their chances of reaching home safely.

They spend their days eating and relaxing in the sunshine; then one day they look up at the sky and decide the sun is getting a bit hot. They quickly pack up and leave for their homes. Once again wave after wave of birds form a v-shaped pattern in the sky as they head homewards. The frozen land they left is green now and there is plenty to eat there too. Back home they soon settle down and after exchanging a few travel stories of lost baggage, bargain-buys and Delhi-bellies, they start thinking about starting a family. When the brief Central Asian summer is over, these chicks and their parents will once more travel back to the warm and friendly lakes of India.

I choose the wrong day to come to Sultanpur lake, though as I walk in I am blissfully unaware about what is going to hit me later. Feeling very pleased with myself, I walk down the mist-covered path and through the curtain of tall grass I see the warm brown feathers of my favourite duck. Despite their long flight the Pintail Ducks are alert even at dawn. Every year, these smart-looking, chocolate brown, grey and white ducks are usually the biggest group on the lake. You will see them either upending in the water or floating about in small groups looking like a bunch of smart, pin-striped corporate guys gathering for an AGM.

They are constantly shifting and twisting, swimming from one end of the lake to the other and then suddenly putting their heads in the water with their pointed tails raised skywards as they search for something to eat. They come out shaking their heads, and quickly look around to make sure the other birds have not grabbed something better and bigger to eat. The ducks usually feed at night and return at dawn to the lake. The adult male ducks like to hang out together in a separate group and can be seen putting their brown heads together to talk business or gossip.

I often try to read their minds and this is what I hear:

'This year the crowd is not very smart. I can see many old fogies on the lake, cluttering up the space. Wish they would retire,' mutters one sleek Pintail Duck to his friend watching a crowd of Greylag Geese float by.

'Yes, I cannot stand these fat geese. They think of nothing but food. No sense of style or any desire to improve their lot. Gobble, gobble all day. What was your bonus package this year?' says the second pintail with a swift shake of his glistening deep chocolate head. They swim a bit and then raise their long elegant necks to look around swiftly as the breeze touches their fine grey and white feathers. To be fair to the Pintail Ducks, they are probably so wary and alert because they were the favourite birds to bag on a duck shoot and thousands were killed just for fun and games on a fine winter morning.

The slow, merry-eyed and pleasantly plump Greylag Geese float past the pintails oblivious of their critical gaze, looking eagerly for a good sunny place to relax and maybe nibble something green and tasty. They are already quite full since the geese like to fly out at night to feed in the fields around the lake and often do a lot of damage to young shoots of wheat and barley. Huge flocks fly out at sunset in stunning v-formations like fighter jets to raid some unfortunate farmer's crop and to feed there all night. They return at dawn to the lake and then spend the day resting and gossiping about the upstart, aggressive pintails.

These two big migratory groups may not hang out together and are very different from each other but they probably take the same long route to get here.

I watch the geese move slowly and gracefully like dignified old ladies, their pink bills gleaming in the gentle winter sunlight. Their wing feathers change from pale grey to silver as the light catches them.

Suddenly, a dark shadow falls on them and there is chaos. With a loud honking sound the geese begin to scatter and I look up to see a Marsh Harrier hovering above our heads.

The only thing that makes the geese move swiftly is the sight of a Marsh Harrier close by. With a splash and a flutter of a hundred wings the birds rise and flee, only to settle down a few minutes later with much grumbling and honking.

The Marsh Harrier, despite its nasty ways, is a recklessly handsome bird I like to watch for hours. It loves to rise high in the air with its wings stretched out and then suddenly it will swoop down to grab a helpless duck. It has a gleaming pale brown head which catches the sunlight as the bird twists and turns in the air. Sometimes it will chase the geese and the ducks just for fun, making them honk hysterically as they rush from one end of the lake to the other. At first you will hear a low long drumbeat as the geese take off and then a loud honking will echo all over the lake as the entire flock rises in the air, screaming abuses at the Marsh Harrier. This handsome hawk is a winter visitor and I wonder if it harasses the geese and ducks in Central Asia too since they both live there in summer.

If you ever have the chance of meeting a Marsh Harrier up close, notice the look of malicious satisfaction in its eyes. It really loves to torment lesser creatures and I sometimes hear its cruel laughter as it soars high up in the sky.

There are smaller groups of other ducks floating about on the lake and it takes me a long time to identify them through the mist. The Mallard is easy because of its green head and yellow beak. But watch out, there is another green-headed duck relaxing next to it and this one is called the Shoveller because of its flat shovel-like bill. You cannot miss the Shoveller and even on a foggy winter morning you will spot its bright mismatched colours. The head is green, the breast white and the underparts a gleaming chestnut. This duck breeds throughout the greater part of Europe, northern Asia as well as North America and many flocks migrate in winter to the Mediterranean, Egypt and Africa. Some prefer to fly down to us and they like it here so much that they hang around much after the other migratory ducks have left for their homes. The Shoveller likes to spend time in small groups or single pairs, feeding in shallow water, the muddier the better. One can see it dipping its head in the water, using its special beak to sieve through mud and muddy water for minute living organisms and aquatic seeds.

I have seen the Shoveller living almost like a tame duck in a small village pond, sharing space happily with the resident buffaloes and often swimming close to people bathing in the pond. It was lucky enough to be never considered worth shooting because of its rank flesh and so it is not wary of humans.

A sudden flash of a russet head tells me that the Red-crested Pochard is also here. This gorgeous duck has flown all the way from Siberia and northern Europe. The male bird is one of the best-looking ducks on the lake with a glossy red head and a crimson bill, shiny black underparts and a glowing white wing-bar. The female is a bit sober and dull-looking but does not seem to mind and swims along her mate, giving him adoring looks. Their dark-headed cousin, the Tufted Pochard, is lurking here amongst the weeds, its tiny yellow eyes gleaming wickedly in the faint light. This duck always reminds me of a villain in a Hindi movie who is waiting for a chance to attack his handsome cousin and grab all his property.

Both the pochards feed on roots and buds of aquatic plants which they get by diving deep underwater. They too feed mostly at night and spend the day swimming about the lake in large groups.

There is a stunning orange-brown duck hiding in one corner—the famous Ruddy Sheldrake, also known as the brahminy duck. These shy creatures come from Ladakh and

Tibet to winter in various water bodies around Delhi as well as other parts of India. Though sometimes their bright orange shape can be seen shining like a rising sun on the waters of the Sultanpur lake, the birds prefer riverine areas and flowing water. I have seen a few pairs on the sandy banks of the Jamuna river and also on the banks of the Ganga near Rishikesh. The ducks feed at night on mostly vegetable matter but they have a strange habit of feeding on different sides of the river.

Why do they separate like this at meal times when all day long they stay really close together? According to folklore, the brahminy ducks are souls of erring lovers cursed by the gods and doomed to remain within sight and hearing of each other but separated at night by a flowing stream across which they call out to each other despairingly. They are called chakwa and chakwi in folk tales from northern India.

Their unusual habits and beautiful orange-chestnut colours have made them a favourite of miniature painters and you will often see them standing next to a pair of love-sick lovers. Sometimes they are painted on the river bank, each keeping to his or her designated side as ordained by the gods.

The other migratory ducks on the lake are the Common Teal, Gadwall and Wigeon. All of these have flown in from their breeding grounds in Central Asia, Siberia and northern Europe. I wonder if the ducks and geese gather in one place before flying out to India. It must be an amazing sight to see thousands of them in one vast group. I will have to travel

Teals on Sultanpur lake.

to Siberia and other remote parts of Central Asia to see this sight. Unlike the brave birds, I lack the stamina and courage and would rather just meet them in the relative comfort of the Sultanpur jheel.

There used to be another duck gliding amongst all these ducks, its beautiful bright pink head an envy of all other birds, but alas, the Pink-headed Duck was last seen in 1935 and is considered extinct now. But you never know, someone might get lucky and spot a blazing pink head one misty, cold morning on the lake and achieve world fame at once.

Just when the call of the water birds, the ripple of wind in the reeds had lulled me to a state of bliss, I am jolted by a scream. The peace and quiet of the lake is shattered as a huge crowd of men, women and children suddenly arrive buzzing like a drone of bees. Again there is a high-pitched scream, which I now realize is the leader of the group laughing.

There are at least a hundred of these people, all carrying banners and wearing red caps which announce '25 Proud Years of FDRC'. Some of them are also carrying umbrellas for some strange reason though the sky is a clear blue. As they jostle past me talking in loud excited voices I ask one woman what FDRC stands for. She looks at me aghast and repeats my question to her companions.

'She is asking what is FDRC.'

'What?' shouts an incredulous lady wearing a jacket which also proclaims '25 Proud Years of FDRC'.

'Are you Indian or from foreign?' the first woman asks me in a hostile voice. The group now comes to a halt and then moves towards me in a tight circle, hundreds of red caps flashing like a French Revolution mob. I hesitate before repeating my innocent question. A few small boys, obviously the progeny of the FDRC women, start throwing stones in the water, scaring the coots and I tell them to stop. 'The birds will get frightened,' I say and the leader calls out in his screeching laugh which reminds me of a Red-billed Blue Magpie's raucous call. 'No birds here, madam, only ducks. Waste of our money.'

The FDRC gang of women and men now come threateningly near me and I am tempted to snatch a cap from the head of one of the rowdy young boys head just to teach them all a lesson so they will not throw stones at birds. But my courage fails and I run away to the safety of the Bird Museum where I know no proud FDRCs will follow me.

The migratory birds quickly move to another end of the

lake where there are no noisy people. They have learnt in the last twenty years that the far end of the lake is much safer and quieter and now stay there mostly. One can walk around the entire lake and at my slow pace I have done it in two hours though my energetic friends take less time. I believe that a birdwatcher has to move slowly, silently and steadily otherwise he or she will miss the sighting. Once I saw a pair of brahminy ducks on this quiet side which my fast moving friends missed and I never let them forget it.

A slight breeze ripples the surface of the lake and the birds float along languidly. Some sleep with their head tucked under their wings while others look around with interest at the landscape. The winter sun warming their backs, abundant vegetarian delights and fish to eat and the company of the other migratory birds obviously makes their long arduous journey worthwhile. Many of them have learnt to ignore noisy crowds of humans and only think of eating well while they are here.

One popular resident, the Spotbill Duck, with bright yellow spots on its beak and flashy orange legs is happy to share the lake with visitors, both humans as well as birds, and never chases the migratory birds away. In fact, I have seen it staying close to the smart and alert pintails as if it was trying to imbibe some of their elegant ways. The snooty pintails, of course, ignore our flashily dressed desi duck and swim past with a cold, indifferent air but the good-natured spotbill does not give up and follows them grinning foolishly.

The coot, a black restless bird, does not like the ducks

and keeps pushing them out of its territory. The coot looks like a small duck but belongs to the rail family and often hangs out with other bad-tempered birds like the colourful Purple Moorhen and its plain-looking cousin, the Indian Moorhen. They may float about the lake like small ducks but their long clumsy legs and ungainly feet give them away as soon as they come out of the water. They look exactly like Cinderella's ugly sisters about to try out the glass slipper unsuccessfully. They fly low over the water, screeching in strident notes, their necks stretched out as if they were trying to win a race.

These water birds can be seen skulking amongst the vegetation, especially where the reeds grow thick and close. They will wait and watch till you come close to them and then rise up in alarm making you feel guilty.

The Bronze-winged Jacana prefers to walk on floating vegetable matter rather than swim and shows off its skill in keeping its balance. Their long toes and claws enable them to walk effortlessly on large leaves picking up aquatic insects and vegetable matter.

Sometimes, right near the edge of the lake, you may find a small brown and white speckled bird running up and down as if preparing for a marathon race. This is the Wood Sandpiper who along with its cousin the Common Sandpiper is spending the winter here to get away from its cold home in the Himalayas. Another similar looking bird is the Little Stint which is the most energetic of all wading birds and can pick up insects at top speed. This bird's brown and white speckled feathers merge into the reeds, pebbles and dry grass on the margins of the lakes but you can see them as soon as they begin to run which is most of the time. They always seem to be in a great hurry to go from one feeding area to another and I think the proverb 'the grass is always greener on the other side' was thought up by a person who had seen these energetic birds.

There are beautiful Flamingoes here gliding in the mist like elegant ballerinas, always stepping around in graceful coordination. Their specialized beaks have to be used with skill—they curve their long necks so that the bill is upside down and can sift food from the shallow water by moving from side to side. Not an easy task but they seem to do it effortlessly and with grace. The only breeding ground they like in India is the remote Rann of Kutch in Gujarat where hundreds of birds gather to build their strange looking mud pie nests on the salt flats.

Behind the slender Flamingoes there is a group of stout White Pelicans floating about slowly and aimlessly like sailboats. Their large powerful beaks are very good for catching fish though I have never seen a bird actually get one. All they seem to do is swim from one end of the lake to the other, pause and then head back. Sometimes you can see an equally stout relative of theirs, the Dalmatian Pelican, in the Delhi zoo but their feathers always look dull unlike the ones in Sultanpur. Their faded look must be a result of the sheer boredom of being in a zoo with nothing to look at except rowdy crowds of humans.

The White Ibis likes to stay near the lake but may suddenly fly off to explore the fields around the water. One can find them standing around in small groups or even alone near village ponds, their lethal-looking curved beaks poised to pick up food. There are three kinds of these birds to be found in winter—the white, black and glossy, each with a pointed, curved beak.

The trees around the lake are full of bird-life too but you have to be careful not to fall into the squelchy mud like I did, trying to get a closer look. As I crashed through the reeds, startling a Purple Moorhen about to sit down for its breakfast, an angry young nilgai rose from the island and headed straight for me. I froze with terror, counting my last moments, pictures from my life flashing past but fortunately he got distracted by a sweet young female nilgai just before he reached me.

The pair stared at each other for a while and then as I rose from the muddy waters, they walked into the sunrise. It took a week for me to scrape the fishy-smelling clay off my shoes and even after that dogs would sniff suspiciously and growl at my feet whenever I wore those unfortunate shoes.

Despite many small but nerve-wracking incidents I still go out every winter to the lake because the sight of the migratory ducks and geese floating on the still, calm water never fails to fascinate me. I am reminded of the Rat's antics from the classic *The Wind in the Willows*:

> And when the ducks stood on their heads suddenly, as ducks will, he would dive down and tickle their necks just under where their chins would be if ducks had chins, till they were forced to come to the surface in a hurry, spluttering and angry and shaking their feathers at him, for it is impossible to say quite all you feel when your head is under water.

During the winter months you may see some smaller birds too like the Bluethroat who has flown down to Delhi from the mountains. The tiny male bird wears a smart blue and chestnut scarf around its little neck and hops about looking for insects under the leaves. It is a friendly bird but because of its tiny size it is not very easy to spot. If you see a pile of dry leaves shaking then wait and watch. The Bluethroat may emerge to greet you with its merry sparkling eyes and a short musical song.

Once a bird came up really close to us and ate a bit of the tomato sandwich we offered it. It stayed with us for a while, cocking its little head as if it wanted to make polite conversation with us or thank us for the tidbit. Then it flew away to search for insects under the tree having had enough of vegetarian fare, I suppose. Its trusting habits worry me and I hope it will have a safe journey home to its breeding grounds far away in Ladakh and Kashmir.

In winter, mustard fields gleam like a sea of yellow on the outskirts of Delhi and this is where the Grey Partridge is running around in circles. It calls out its well-known notes, repeating whatever it is saying over and over again. The reason for this agitated call is that partridges love being in touch with their mates and feel insecure if they find themselves alone. The reason for this anxiety is probably because they have been shot relentlessly over the past centuries. In villages their notes are compared to noon-tel-adrak which means salt-oil-ginger.

I once went birdwatching with a friend whose husband was in the police. Her driver, also a policeman, suddenly leapt out of the car, and caught a fleeing partridge by its legs.

'What is the point of watching them, better to be catching them,' he said, offering us the bird with a smart salute. He was very disappointed when we made him release the bird, who, although shocked, was alive and well and scampered off quickly into the safety of the shrubs. The bird will probably boast endlessly to its friends about how brave it was and how well it fought to save its life.

A birdwatcher is often treated with scorn by people who feel we are wasting our time just watching birds.

'You should catch and eat them,' said an old friend from Nepal. She had eaten most of the birds from my bird guide and suggested recipes for many of them.

'The jungle fowl is best roasted with ginger and the quail is delicious if you do a dry masala fry,' she said, drooling over my bird book.

The Common Quail knows how much my friend would like to turn it into a spicy curry and hides in the grassy meadows, as still as a rock. It will wait till you almost tread on its tail and then suddenly fly off in a great flurry of feathers.

A rather plump and cheerful cousin of the partridge is the chukor—a favourite of Indian poets and miniature painters. It is the symbol of love in miniature paintings and a single bird always signifies a lonely, love-sick lover pining away for his or her beloved.

A very attractive and elusive bird which very few people ever saw was the Himalayan quail. It was last seen sometime in 1876 and though many ornithologists keep looking for this elusive bird, it is sadly considered to be extinct.

Winter days, though grey and bleak, are the perfect time to make a short trip to the Keoladeo Ghana National Park in Bharatpur in Rajasthan, less than 200 kilometres from Delhi. As soon as you arrive you will find lorikeets, a country cousin of the parakeets, swinging from the trees. For some reason these dumpy green birds like to hang upside down from the branches like skilled trapeze artistes. Sometimes I have seen them lurking on a jamun tree in the company of Blossom-headed Parakeets but these well-behaved birds always look embarrassed and try their best to feed on the topmost branch of the tree so no one can associate them with their wayward relatives swinging upside-down.

At Bharatpur, once you go deep into the marshy lakes surrounded by acacia, neem and jamun trees, you will see hundreds of migratory ducks, geese and cranes. This is where the rare Siberian Crane likes to come for a winter break and it is a thrilling sight to see the long-legged, red-faced birds feeding in the lake, totally relaxed and at home in their new surroundings, thousands of miles away from their frozen breeding grounds in Siberia. The arrival of these famous cranes is always greeted with great joy by bird enthusiasts all over India. Their relatives, the Demoiselle Crane and the Common Crane all travel together in huge flocks from their frozen homes in Eastern Siberia. Hugh Whistler, a famous British ornithologist and police officer, who was fortunate enough to witness this amazing sight in 1928, writes:

> In North-west India the passage is an impressive sight. Both species appear to travel together. The observer who is favourably situated will hear one morning a loud clanging call and looking towards the sound will see in the distant sky a vast tangled skein of birds. As it approaches it resolves itself into an immense concourse of Cranes flying at a tremendous height. The stream of birds travels across the sky like an army. Big flocks, small parties, single birds and chevrons extend as far as the eye can reach, all travelling in the same line. Then the leading flock circles round in a vast swirl, feeling for its direction; the next formations close up to it and again the army moves forward. As they go a single bird trumpets, answered by others.

Once returning from Bharatpur by train, I saw a large group of Demoiselle Cranes feeding in a field. As the train passed by they all raised their beautiful heads and watched, then just before I lost sight of the cranes, I heard a powerful, sonorous call as if the birds were trying to match the train's shrill whistle. Thrilled with the sight, I pointed it out to my fellow passengers—a young couple and the man's mother.

'All very well to see birds but do you know it is an ill omen to see them at sunset?' announced the elderly lady. 'I thought it was unlucky to see owls, these looked like some big white birds,' said her daughter-in-law. The lady fixed her with a cold look and then turned to me and said, 'It is the habit of young people these days to talk rubbish and contradict everything. When I was young if my mother-in-law said night was day I would always agree.' There was a short pause and then the daughter-in-law, a feisty young girl, smiled at her mother-in-law, 'Well, those days are long gone. I think we should speak the truth. I know owls are unlucky and these birds were certainly not owls. I am very sure about that. You tell me, since you seem to know all about birds. Were they owls or not?' She looked at me belligerently. I did not want to get involved in what seemed like a long-drawn family battle and opened my book.

'Those days may have gone but good manners and respect for elders still remain—at least in girls from good families,' said ma-in-law, opening a box of sweets and offering me one. 'Home-made and not shop bought,' she said. It was obviously a bribe and I shamelessly took it. 'Good manners and respect for elders is very important,' I said, swallowing the delicious laddoo and the son, who had been looking out of the window, pretending he was not a part of this feud, smiled gratefully at me. 'Yes, yes be polite to each and everyone, man, woman and child—that should be our national motto,' he muttered, not looking at his wife. We all munched silently in the uneasy truce but I could see the young daughter-in-law planning her revenge. She had a 'wait-till-you-get-home' look on her pretty face while her husband fixed his gaze firmly out of the window.

This squabbling young couple were certainly not like the beautiful Sarus Crane—these birds are totally devoted to each other and mate for life. It is believed that if one bird dies, the other will pine away for it. The Sarus Crane is very tall, almost more than five feet, and you can see the handsome stately pair standing around in fields near villages where they know no one will ever harm them. I was lucky enough once to see their courtship dance. Each bird bows, takes a little jump in the air and stretching out its wings, begins to dance around the other, always making eye contact. They dance like this for about ten minutes and then stop. Once you have seen this amazing dance it will stay with you forever.

At least, that is what I thought. The friends who were also in the car with me watching this amazing dance, thought the birds were fighting. 'They are trying to kill each other, must be rivals,' said one. 'I think the big fellow is having a fit. Do birds have psychological problems?' said another. 'Some ants must have got into their feathers,' said the third. 'They are trying to shake them off.'

If you spend a week in Bharatpur National Park you will notice that every day the population of the jheel increases by leaps and bounds, as more and more birds land on the lake. They look very pleased with themselves and I can hear

Little Cormorant on Sultanpur Lake

them heaving a collective sigh of relief and congratulating each other for reaching Bharatpur safely after such a long and arduous trip.

Garganey Teals, Ruddy Shelducks, Gadwalls, Wigeons, Shovellers and Red-crested Pochards all swim in close groups, happy to share the abundant supply of aquatic food. Some catch up on their sleep since they have been out feeding all night while others float around, enjoying the warm sunshine. Soon they will be joined by hundreds of Pintailed Ducks, Barheaded and Greylag Geese and the noise level around the lake will increase dramatically.

As I walk around, surrounded by a babble of birdcalls, suddenly there is a loud shrill cry. I stop in my tracks wondering if someone has fallen in the water. I take a few steps following the sound and arrive in front of a tall acacia tree that is trembling with discordant bird cries. On every branch sits a water-bird eyeing its neighbour with a not-so-friendly look. There are Little Cormorants, Darters and a few Little Egrets. The birds are all screaming loudly for some reason and though I look around I cannot see any predator birds nearby. One member of this group has a good reason to vent its anger on the world. The Little Egret is a very common bird now found near ponds, lakes and often seen running behind a farmer as he ploughs his fields. But in the nineteenth and twentieth centuries, these long-legged white birds were hunted relentlessly for their beautiful breeding plumage called aigrettes which every fashionable lady wanted. Thousands of egrets were killed and they almost became extinct. Fortunately the fad died out and the bird is still living happily with us.

The Darter, an unfriendly angry-looking bird, also called the snakebird because of its long neck, is an expert at catching fish and can stay underwater for quite some time. I saw it dive in once and waited with bated breath, counting—it came out only when I reached fifty-eight. It had a small fish in its beak which it shook with a triumphant air and then swallowed whole.

Though Bharatpur, with its shaded lanes and vast lakes is a wonderful place to see water-bird colonies, huge flocks of migratory ducks and geese, there are many other birds here, too. Walking along the shady bunds which run along the lakes, many woodland birds are just waiting to be seen.

The rare and secretive Collared Scops Owl is here, hiding on an old jamun tree. The brown, grey-and-black design on its chest and wings enable it to merge perfectly with the bark of the tree and unless you look very carefully you may miss it. The Indian Nightjar is also the same colouring but since it begins to call as soon as dusk falls it can be seen sitting on the road, its ruby-red eyes gleaming when the car's headlights falls on it.

Besides an amazing variety of water and woodland birds, this national park has many hidden areas which are the favourite habitats of jackals and their ugly friends, the hyenas. There are rocky dry places where the mongoose hides and pools with old and wise turtles. There are pythons too.

On one trip, my friends had seen enough birds so we moved away from the lake towards the dry dusty fields in search of the famous reptile. 'Always more interesting to see a big fat snake than these brown ducks,' they said.

Our guide, a very knowledgeable young man called Tara, began telling us fascinating stories about old times when Bharatpur was a popular shooting spot for maharajas. His grandfather was a beater and almost lost an arm when a British guest's gun went off accidently. 'He was not badly hurt, just grazed by the bullet, but the sahib who shot him was so upset that he fainted when he saw the blood oozing from my grandfather's arm. My father had to carry both him and my grandfather back to the hotel. The poor sahib did not stop crying and gave my father a lot of money. My grandmother bought two new cows with the money and became famous in our village since he was the first person to receive a letter from England. The sahib sent him a box of biscuits too which he never ate since they had egg in them someone said. He gave it to the cows. We still have the box though.'

We were in a lonely, remote area of Bharatpur now. There were sandy, uneven paths going nowhere and behind a line of wild date palms, the sun was slowly getting ready to set. Far away the birds were calling out to each other as they too got ready to roost on their favourite trees or watery corners. A gentle scent of wild flowers floated in the air. All was calm and peaceful.

'Look, there is a python,' Tara said casually, pointing to a glistening pile on the ground. We jumped back a few feet and then watched the gleaming coil as it moved a bit. Another guide appeared with two tourists, a Swedish couple, followed by a small village boy. Our young friend, chewing on a stick of babool, said, 'Python snake can squeeze a fat man or a woman to death in a few minutes.' Though he had spoken in Hindi, the Swedish couple moved back even further. Tara explained that most of the time the snake wanted only a juicy hare or fat rodent and was harmless if left alone. The boy narrowed his eyes, chewed a bit and said, 'My sister's husband was attacked the other day,' and repeated his words in English for the benefit of the visitors.

'By python…this one…attack?' the couple said in one voice. It was difficult to imagine that this plump, sedentary creature so content in its dusty hollow would ever have the energy to attack anything.

'No no, by a leopard. There are many leopards here in the forest. They often take cows away and attack people too. One foreigner lady was attacked last month,' said the boy, staring at the Swedish couple who were now looking very worried.

'No sir, no one was attacked,' said Tara and gave the boy a stern look. The other guide began scolding him in the local dialect and we caught some strong words.

The boy was clearly enjoying himself and nothing would stop him.

'My grandfather said he saw a man being dragged into the lake by a crocodile,' he said with a grin.

'There are crocodiles here? We thought only ducks and geese,' murmured the Swedes in a low whisper.

'No, no only turtle, water fowl and fish,' said our guide trying to get the party to move ahead. The boy followed and began a long story about his grandfather's sudden death by drowning in the very lake we were heading for.

'He was trapped by the water hyacinth. They say there is a water monster living in there who drags people to their death on certain days of the week.'

'On which days?' we asked, quite mesmerized by this young lad.

'What day is today?' asked the boy.

'Tuesday,' we said.

'Then you are safe. It only comes out on Thursdays and Saturdays,' said the boy and scampered off laughing. We walked quickly as the sun sank behind us, the birds fell silent and in the gathering dusk, every sound now held a menace.

I thought of the great python Kaa from Kipling's *Jungle Book:*

> Then Kaa came straight, quickly and anxious to kill. The fighting strength of a python is in the driving blow of his head backed by all the strength and weight of his body. If you can imagine a lance, or a battering-ram, or a hammer weighing nearly half a ton driven by a cool, quiet mind living in the handle of it, you can roughly imagine what Kaa was like when he fought. A python four or five feet long can knock a man down if he hits him fairly in the chest, and Kaa was thirty feet long, as you know... Kaa was everything that the monkeys feared in the jungle, for none of them knew the limits of his power, none of them could look him in the face, and none had ever come out alive out of his hug.

We had almost reached the end of the forest path when a lone Demoiselle Crane, about to retire for the night, called out a trumpet-like farewell note and then the nightjar began its gentle, sweet evening song which would last all night. Bharatpur was safe and peaceful once more.

In Delhi, the winter days march on. The sun is sulking all day and suddenly sets without warning. The darkness falls without any announcement of dusk. We drink cinnamon and ginger tea, munch peanuts to keep warm and many of us make new quilts or re-thrash the cotton-wool from old ones. I often hear the cotton-thrashers and quilt-makers working away behind my house, their harp-like wooden thrashers twanging away like a happy jazz band. One day I see a tailorbird flying away with little bits of cotton. This far-sighted bird is stealing materials for its nest and though spring and nest building are still far away, the bird is making the most of a cold winter's day. It is probably her way (it was a female bird) of keeping warm and it helped me to think of spring too, waiting in the wings, shivering in the cold and hoping its time to emerge would come soon. The trees wait patiently, buds hold their breath and soon, any day now, they will feel the gentle touch of spring on their petals and know it is time to flower.

SPRING

But the sun gains power in the south-east.
It changes the mist into a fleeting garment,
Not of cold or of warm grey, but of diaphanous gold

~ EDWARD THOMAS

With tumbled hair of swarms of bees
And flower-robes dancing in the breeze
With sweet, unsteady lotus-glances,
Intoxicated Spring advances.

~ AMARU

The gentle spring sunlight dances playfully on the leaves, moving swiftly from one tree-top to another as if searching for a playmate. The days are gradually emerging from their winter blues, along with thousands of buds, shoots and wild flowers. Butterflies, newly freed from their chrysalis, now carefully stretch their delicate wings—a bit hesitant to fly just yet.

The temperature is perfect in Delhi, and the air is scented with a strange perfume of hidden flowers. Everyone is grateful for this weather because those who live in Delhi know that this golden spell will not last long and soon, in just a few weeks, this gentle sunlight will turn around to sting them with its fierce rays.

For now, the beautiful sunlight is as soothing as a balm made of healing herbs. The air is as clean as it ever will be and the winter fog, tinged with wood-smoke, has disappeared to its secret hide-out till next year. There is a faint, lingering chill in the early morning breeze but it carries a warm, spicy scent, telling us that it is turning away from winter and looking towards summer.

Children, suddenly feeling lighter after having shed their heavy winter woollens, scamper around in the parks which were lonely and deserted during the cold, grey days. I went for a walk just a few days ago at sunset and the mist suddenly came down like a muslin cloth to drape every tree. I could see nothing except for a few shimmering car lights and behind me a lone evening walker's footsteps echoed on the pavement. Suddenly I felt like Sherlock Holmes following a murderer in Victorian London.

Trees gradually come out of their grey winter mood, shaking off their lethargy bit by bit and then by the middle of February they are at their sparkling best. Not just the trees of Delhi but plants and birds, office babus and hawkers, housewives, visiting tourists, marching protesters, shopping NRIs and carefree children all bask in the gentle sunshine which slowly spreads its warm, soothing light all over the city.

Everyone remembers the long, miserable winter when the short days were cold and bleak with a fog descending from noon to sunset, so every bit of sunshine is welcome. In the beginning the sun is not sure of its strength and comes out in sudden bursts then retreats shyly leaving people shivering once more. But as the days go by, the sun becomes stronger and shows itself for a few hours longer and people rush out to greet it as if it were a long-lost friend.

Now, all day, the parks and roundabouts are crowded with people trying to catch some of this spring sunshine. At noon hundreds of government babus sunbathe in the gardens near India Gate. In fact, some areas are strictly reserved by an unwritten rule for bonafide government servants. I tried once to intrude into one of these charmed circles and was accosted at once by a lady. 'Which department? Accounts... agriculture...culture?' she asked, narrowing her eyes. She could see I was not from any of these departments and needed to be chased away at once. Serious card sessions go on while some just snooze in the delicious sunlight with a newspaper covering the face. I have often seen people getting official documents signed and stamped in these open-air offices. The head of the department, always a portly gentleman, sits on a folded blanket to give him an elevated position while his juniors sit on the grass.

In residential colonies women gather in small groups to knit sweaters and gossip while their children play in the sunshine. You can see garlands of cauliflowers, carrots and turnips drying in the gentle sun. These vegetables, so plentiful now, will be in short supply in summer and then these garlands will be used to cook delicious dishes to remind everyone of spring.

In some parks trainee sadhus hold sessions, offering free spiritual advice to passersby. A palmist may also set up his business to read the future of any ambitious babu worried about the promotion. And to feed these large groups there are peanut sellers forever present, armed with large supplies of chopped onions and chillies.

Some mornings are still very cold, as if winter is not letting go of Delhi but the sun asserts itself and by noon, it gets a beautiful warm, golden patina. The sky is a delicate shade of soft blue which we do not ever get to see the rest of the year. In summer the Delhi sky is a burning brass and copper plate while in winter it turns grey and during the rains a dark, mysterious blue with streaks of brilliant silver.

To celebrate the blue skies and the perfect spring light, a trio of trees decides to blossom. Putting the memories of the foggy and cold days behind them, these tall, handsome trees hold a short discussion with each other and then order their buds to get ready. They do all this work quietly and stealthily like elves in a fairy tale and you will not be able to see the buds unless you climb up the tree.

Each of the three trees claims it is the most beautiful of flowering trees and feels it is it right to be the first one to bring out the blossoms. Usually, the magnificent silk-cotton is first.

This tree opens the flower show, followed by the equally gorgeous flame of the forest and then the elegant coral tree shyly joins the parade. The buds appear on the trees by the end of January or the first week of February and then as the golden sunshine of the brief spring days beams down benevolently on them, the trees begin the display of their flowers one by one and Delhi is overwhelmed by spring fever.

All three trees love the colour red and their blossoms are in various shades of red and orange. Standing a few feet taller than most other trees along the roadside, the silk-cotton is a great show-off—you cannot pass by this tree without admiring its flowers. The branches reach high up into the sky as if offering the flowers to the sky but most of them quickly fall on the ground below. Cup-shaped with five

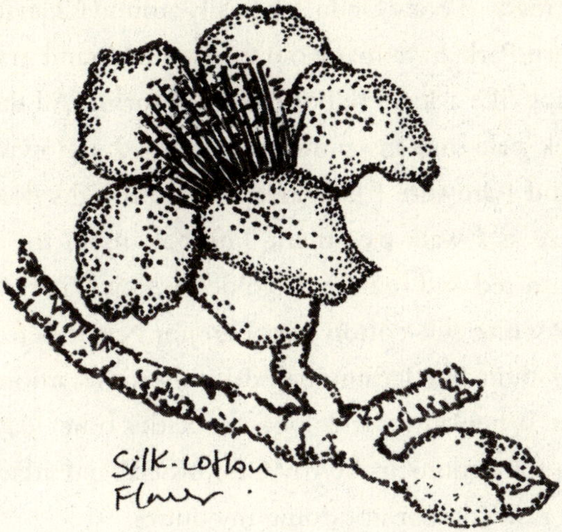

fleshy petals formed around a dense cluster of tall stamens, the flowers look spectacular but have no fragrance. In fact, ancient Indian sages found this tree useless and a braggart since it only produced flamboyant flowers but gave no edible fruit. They named it dushta druma to vent their irritation on the unfortunate tree.

However, squirrels, goats, deer and birds love the flowers and so do cows who will eat the plump buds with great relish. I have seen sunbirds, parakeets, Coppersmiths, mynas, White-eyes, owls and woodpeckers flying around or sitting on a silk-cotton tree. Some birds are there for the nectar while others drop in for a few insects. Squirrels always gather in large groups to feast on the large flowers and, very often, if you happen to stand under a large silk-cotton in flower, you will find half-eaten flowers falling on your head.

The roads of New Delhi, especially around Chanakyapuri and Nehru Park, have many old trees which stand grand and tall, blazing like a small hill of colour in spring. All the other trees look pale and insignificant next to the glowing silk-cotton and I am sure I have heard envious sighs floating in the breeze as I walk past them. The colours of the flowers range from red and orange to golden yellow. There used to be a rare white silk-cotton near Sarojini Nagar before Dilli Haat was built but I cannot find it any more amongst the buildings. When I went to look for it the other day, I was mistaken for a municipality (MCD) official and attacked by the local residents for not doing my duties.

'Mosquitoes breeding everywhere...you never come to check,' shouted an angry old gentleman.

'I was looking for a tree,' I said.

'Tree...what tree? Too many trees here...that is why wild animals are coming into our homes. I saw a mongoose here yesterday.'

'It had big white flowers,' I tried again.

'No trees here with flowers. Only a jungle with mongoose and mosquitoes,' said the old man, pointing an accusing finger at me.

I will try again soon because I am sure the rare silk-cotton is still there somewhere flowering away secretly behind a barat ghar or a Mother Dairy booth.

The flowers of the silk-cotton gradually turn into fruit pods and though they are not edible for humans, they contain a soft cotton called semal. As spring marches on swiftly and the days turn warmer, the tree sheds its flowers and changes from brilliant orange red to a canopy of green. Now you will find tiny green pods on the branches. These will soon burst open to scatter puffs of fluffy cotton all over the streets.

Families of cotton gatherers set up camp under each tree. They bring down the seed pods with long bamboo poles and then each seed pod is carefully deseeded and strands of cotton wool taken out. The silky cotton is too soft to be spun and can only be used to stuff pillows and cushions. These are sold at a good price by the semal-gatherer families to people passing by on the road. The mother stitches the pillow cases and the father and the older children gather the semal and stuff each pillow case. 'This semal pillow will give you good sleep, cure headaches and backaches,' announces the mother to a crowd, waving a newly-made pillow. Her message convinces many passersby and they quickly buy a colourful pillow or two and walk away, hoping to sleep better that night. I too buy one, though my problem is not insomnia but keeping awake.

I gave a freshly-made, hand-stitched semal pillow to a friend who had just got married. Her husband of one week apparently broke out in a fit of sneezing as soon as he put his head on the pillow. His eyes watered and nose ran copiously, ruining their honeymoon and putting a strain on their future marital relationship. She quickly bought him a synthetic, foam pillow and saved their marriage, though I do not believe the poor silk-cotton was to blame.

The second tree in the orange-red group is the flame

of the forest. This handsome tree is not really fond of Delhi but there are a few old trees in Buddha Jayanti Park, Nehru Park, the Delhi Zoo and Shantivan which offer us a glorious display of flowers. At first the brown-green buds look all unhappy and crumpled as if some giant's hand had crushed them. But one day, from their soft, velvety green sepals, a small orange petal peeps out. Then, day by day, the orange takes over the velvet sepal cups and finally one morning the beautiful flowers emerge in their full glory.

Each flower is shaped like the orange beak of a parakeet though some pessimists say they look like blood-drenched claws. Soon the branches are laden with dense clusters of bright orange flowers and from afar the tree looks as if it is on fire, hence the name. To truly appreciate the name one must see vast groves of these fiery-orange trees blazing in the forests of the Terai region of Uttar Pradesh.

Many Sanskrit shlokas mention the beauty of this tree, called kimsuka in Sanskrit. Its Hindi name is dhak and palas. The poet Kalidas wrote that when the tree is in full blossom, the earth looks like a bride bedecked in her orange-red garments. The sufi poet Amir Khusru likened the flowers to a lion's claws stained with blood. According to a myth, it sprung from the feather of a falcon which was dipped in soma—the favourite beverage of the gods.

Buddhists consider this tree sacred and ancient texts say that Queen Maha Maya clutched a branch of the palas tree when Lord Buddha was born.

The tree generously flowers just around the festival of

Holi and the pretty orange flowers are made into a yellow dye which is used to make an organic colour that may not be very bright but is gentle on the skin. The flowers were used to dye the robes of Buddhist monks in ancient India and prayer flags are still dyed in a vat full of flame of the forest blossoms. The leaves of the tree are stitched into plates by tribal people and I remember eating bhog in a temple where the food was served on these leaf-plates. When we finished we fed the plates and the leftover food to the cows who were waiting patiently outside. This was long before thermocol plates arrived and no one has yet invented an edible plate for either cows or us.

Parakeets like to nibble on the young buds of the flame of the forest, striking dramatic poses on the flower-laden branches. Purple Sunbirds too hover around the tree though I am not sure what they are searching for since the flowers do not seem to have a good supply of nectar but then birds always seem to know what they are doing. The only exception are male sparrows who often mistake their reflection in the window panes for a rival and begin a long and belligerent argument.

The third member of the orange-red club appears with a display of brilliant colour towards the end of spring. The coral tree's blossoms are shaped like tiny curved wings and appear quickly as the spring days go by. First, you will see a cluster of velvety green buds at the end of each leafless branch. These look like tiny leaves but then one fine spring morning you are taken by surprise as a sparkling parade of orange flowers appears on the tree. The flowers grow close together and the shades of orange, crimson and red petals merge and dance as the light changes. The leaves of the coral tree are heart-shaped and called trimurti, since they are in the form of three leaflets. Vishnu is represented by the middle leaflet and Brahma by the left while Shiva is the right leaflet. The leaves of the flame of the forest are also called trimurti in praise of the three gods.

The coral can be easily grown from a cutting and quickly grows into an elegant tree which gives plenty of shade in summer, beautiful flowers in spring and remains bare in winter. It meets all the requirements of a farmer and is planted in all the tea gardens of Assam. It allows the tea shrubs to bask in sunlight when required and remain cool in the shade when the days get hot. In tea gardens you can see tiny flowerpeckers hovering over the coral flowers, their brightly coloured yellow, green and red feathers matching the petals. Many other birds love the nectar-filled flowers as well as tiny insects that live on the branches. On a good day you may see babblers, mynas, crows, drongos, wren-warblers, tailorbirds, bulbuls and tree-pies on the tree.

I think these three beautiful flowering trees bring out their orange-red flowers one after the other just to confuse us. The only way to recognize each one is to carefully examine their flowers. The silk-cotton is red and orange but cup-shaped, the flame of the forest is red and orange too, but the flowers are curved and grow in a spike. The coral is again red and orange but each flower is pointed and grows close

together in a bract. Their leaves are shaped differently too. The silk-cotton has lance-shaped compound palmate leaves arranged like the fingers on your palm while the flame of the forest and the coral have a three leaflet formation.

In Delhi, the Purple Sunbird—a tiny bird with a sharp beak—is very fond of the coral blossom though its favourite is the delicate, orchid-like flowers of the kachnar. In the mating season the male sunbird acquires a dark shiny purple breeding plumage, while the female remains a sober greenish brown as always. The tiny, restless bird hunts insects all day and suddenly breaks into a squeaky song as if very pleased with itself. It is very easy to spot when the male is all dressed up in its shiny metallic purple and dark blue feathers though the female gets lost in the green foliage of the kachnar.

The kachnar is an elegant tree and was a great favourite of miniature painters. It can be seen forming the background to many Kangra miniature paintings. When the tree is in flower it looks so beautiful that the Sanskrit name for it is vanarajah, or king of the forest. The flowers of the kachnar are orchid-like and have five long curved petals. Each petal has a fine pattern of veins which make it look translucent in the sunlight. It is part of the Bauhinia family. The flowers of various kinds of Bauhinia range from pure white to crimson pink and the most beautiful trees are seen on the lower foothills of the Himalayas where the trees grow much taller than in Delhi. You will see the flower-bedecked tree sparkling on the hillside like a huge bouquet of orchids. They have a faint lavender-like scent which does not last long and floats away in the breeze like a faint memory.

The leaves of the kachnar are shaped like two kidneys

joined together and it is because of this twin formation that the tree got its botanical name Bauhinia in honour of the famous sixteenth-century twin botanists Casper and Jan Bauhin.

I do not know if the famous twins ever tasted the pickle made with the green buds of kachnar but it is very popular in many north Indian homes. A curry is made with the tender flowers and buds and you can see the buds being sold in heaps in vegetable markets though I always hesitate to buy them. Think of how many flowers you are eating in each mouthful.

As the gentle days of spring continue to sparkle, the mango tree brings out its spikes of fragrant blossoms. They may not be as pretty as the other spring blossoms but they attract lots of insects with their sweet nectar. These are called manjari in Hindi and were often mentioned in Sanskrit poetry since they were considered to be Cupid's darts.

Parakeets, whether in love or not, are always around when the mango begins to flower and the Purple Sunbirds too often drop by to feed on the mango tree. There is a heady scent floating around the tree which attracts insects and insect-eating birds. With bees hovering around the flowers, it seems the tree is humming all day.

Mango blossoms, bees and the spring breeze appear in these lines by the great twelfth-century poet Jayadeva to describe the heartache Radha suffers when separated from Krishna in his epic poem *Gita Govinda*:

> Breeze from a lakeside garden
> Coaxing buds on new asoka branches
> Into clusters of scarlet flowers
> Is fanning the flames to burn me.
> Of new mango blossoms
> Humming with roving bumblebees
> Is no comfort to me now, friend.

One can spend hours under a mango tree since there are always birds dropping by to meet you. Once, stranded due to a flat tyre under an old mango tree in the foothills, I was lucky enough to see Scarlet Minivets hunting for insects, an adult Paradise Flycatcher swinging its lovely long tail as it thought up a cunning plan to outwit a crow, and a shy Golden Oriole hiding quietly in the dense green foliage. Next to them a pair of Wood Pigeons whispered secrets to each other, or maybe they were just discussing their travel plans since these restless birds—a distant cousin of the familiar Grey Pigeon—are always on the move in search of better feeding grounds. They do not believe in solitary holidays and always move in flocks creating a flutter amongst other birds with their noise and chatter very much like big groups of tourists who love to talk about everything they have seen or are going to see or have missed seeing.

The golden mild days of spring go by so swiftly. Much as one tries to think of ways to hold on to them, nothing will stop the sun from getting stronger each day. Summer is waiting in the wings in its armour of burning gold, all ready to take over from gentle spring.

Kalidas often wrote in praise of spring and in his play *Kumarasambhava* he made Spring an important character who helps Kama, the god of love, in his quest to make Shiva fall in love with Uma as wished by the gods:

> And then within these mountain-forest reaches,
> Skilled to distract saint's thoughts from heaven above
> The young awakening Spring now yawns and
> stretches,
> Beloved companion of the god of love.
> The ashok then, its trunk and branches laden,
> Full-flowered with foil of many a green leaf-shoot
> Impatient, quite forgot to expect a maiden
> To wake its flowers with ankle-tinkling foot.

The ashok tree is a symbol of spring and according to mythology, it is so sensitive that it will only flower if a beautiful maiden touches it with her foot. The elegant, almost evergreen tree, which brings out newly polished leaves in spring, is said to take away grief in Indian folklore. It is planted in many parks and gardens and its crown of glossy, pointed leaves can be seen gleaming in the spring sunlight. This is when the tiny hidden flowers appear too and are worshipped, along with the leaves, during the festival of Chaitra.

There is another smaller tree called ashok which has similar leaves but orange-red flowers and is not very common in Delhi. I would always confuse the two till I read Pradip Krishen's informative book *Trees of Delhi*, in which he points out the difference. He calls the smaller tree the Sita-Ashok and I think this is the one which is considered a symbol of chastity. In the epic Ramayana, Sita sat in a grove of ashok trees and remained virtuous all the time she was held a prisoner by Ravana in Lanka. Buddhists also consider this tree to be sacred and plant it in many monasteries. Gautama Buddha's mother Queen Maha Maya retired to a grove of ashok trees when she went into labour and it is said Lord Buddha was born under this sacred tree in Lumbini.

As spring glides along, making the days warmer, most gardens in Delhi are filled with flowers and even the parks are what every newspaper hack cannot resist calling 'a riot of colours'. Jagannath, my old mali, is very proud of what he calls angrezi flowers and refuses to plant my favourite marigolds. These pretty orange and yellow flowers may not win prizes at garden shows but are filled with medicinal values and if you plant a few marigolds near your house, they will keep insects away.

Maybe that is why they are used in temples, weddings and funerals—a wise choice made by our ancient sages to give the marigold religious status so that it is used whenever there are too many people around.

Parakeets love to nibble these flowers, eating each petal delicately, as if it was the most delicious snack but other birds seem to ignore it except for an odd lame crow I knew. It would settle down in one shady corner of my garden clutching a marigold clumsily in its claw and then begin to nibble gracefully. It would look up from time to time, roll its eyes like a food critic, savouring each orange-gold petal. The other insect-munching crows would watch and heckle this vegetarian outsider in their clan, but the organic-food loving crow nibbled on ignoring their jibes. It survived on this marigold diet for many years and could out-hop the cats in the garden.

The English garden flowers are seen everywhere one goes in Delhi at this time. You can admire phlox, petunias, pansies, dahlias, nasturtiums, sweet-peas, geraniums and holyhocks. Even the smallest patch of green will have at least one or two of these angrezi flowers. Most people who have a garden get very competitive around this time and I know many gardeners who inject vitamins into their pansies or geraniums to make them bigger and brighter. Nothing will ruin a friendship more than the words 'my petunias are better and bigger than yours' or 'look at my imported double-dahlia, your desi ones are a bit small, aren't they?'

Jagannath, our mali, belongs to an old family of highly

qualified gardeners from Uttar Pradesh and does exactly what he thinks is right. He insists on planting the flowers in a neat, military-like row. When I ask him to mix them up to make them look more 'English cottage garden' style which means a carefully cultivated natural look, he refuses. 'This is how the flowers should grow. Tall ones at the back, short ones in the middle and the little ones in front. My father and my grandfather told me this is how it should be done,' he says with a firm shake of the khurpi.

Year after year we battle on and one winter I stole out at dawn and replanted the seedlings in an untidy row. Jagannath saw what I had done but did not comment. Next day, the poor seedlings had been replanted in neat rows. 'I told you, they must grow according to their height,' he said to me in a headmaster-like voice and then spat out a stream of paan juice to declare the matter had ended. So the flowers grew in an orderly fashion, winter after winter, except for an odd pansy or petunia which escaped the regimented line and played truant just to please me.

The best case of truant flowers are to be seen on the hillsides of Kasauli. A hundred years ago a kind English lady, who was very fond of gardening, planted dahlia. I am sure her mali made sure they were grown in neat rows. But gradually the plants grew weary of being confined to their little garden and began to escape one by one. They crept out into the misty dawn and sank their delicate roots in the rich soil of the hillsides. There they grew amongst the wild flowers, and ferns, happy at last to be free of the dreaded line. Today, if you go to Kasauli in September after the rainy season when all the other wild plants sprout in the mountains, you can see thousands of dahlias of every colour and size on the hillsides.

When Charles Metcalfe, Governor of Agra and known as the 'King of Delhi' by fellow countrymen, suddenly came upon a host of English flowers on a hillside in Kasauli in 1827, he was overwhelmed and wrote in a letter home:

> Nature is here in luxurious fecundity—the hills are covered with trees and shrubs and flowers—what delights us Indians most is to see the earliest acquaintances of our Infancy, on which we have not before set eyes since we quitted England—daisies, buttercups, nettles, dandelions, etc. strawberries, raspberries, roses growing wild with larkspur, columbine, violets, etc. and the oak too, the leaf different from ours, but the acorn the same.

Little did he know that a hundred years later all these flowers would grow happily in the gardens of Delhi.

The English flowers in Delhi have a brief spell of glory during spring and as soon as the days begin to get warmer they give a collective sigh and then quietly wilt and die. Some brave ones carry on for a week or so longer, the petunias amongst them putting on a brave, colourful display like gladiators saluting Caeser before they died.

This is the time the birds get busy picking up the seeds or attacking the insects and worms that lurk under the rotting sweet-peas, cornflowers and pansies. There is a bird that roams in the garden all day now amongst the dying petunias and pansies. It is the Coucal—a handsome black and rust-coloured bird with an identity crisis. Also known as the crow pheasant, the Coucal behaves like a small animal instead of a bird. You will rarely see it fly though it does know how to do so. It spends all day running in the shadows of the garden in a strange furtive manner as if it had done something wrong and was hiding its guilty secret from the other birds. I have a resident bird in my garden and very often I see it brooding in a dark, weed-filled corner, its eyes gleaming with remorse.

Sometimes it picks up an insect or two but never shows any joy in eating like other birds do. The crows dislike the Coucal though they are distant cousins and keep challenging it to come out in the open and fight them like a 'man'. But the Coucal just hunches its wings and goes deeper into the debris of dead flowers. As soon as spring is over, it will disappear into the Ridge forest. It would like to walk there, but it knows the dangers on the way from crows and traffic so it makes an effort and flies away on its clumsy wings.

The warmer days bring out a gang of insect-loving Large Grey Babblers and the noisy group gathers every morning in my garden to have a feast. At first I hear them discussing their plans at great length with many arguments and heated words. Then finally they decide on a course of action and all seven take a short flight to the corner of the garden where the flowers have turned into seed pods and various insects are lurking. At first they rustle through the dead leaves and pick up food silently—but not for long. One of the sisters says something under her breath and immediately the others have to reply. Sometimes their relatives, the Jungle Babblers, also join the party and then there is a full blown argument shattering the peace of the garden. I can hear them say to each other:

'Why do you always contradict me?'

'You are the one who starts the argument. I was quietly eating my beetle.'

'YOU came into my space, as always.'

'I am fed up of this constant bickering. I will go to my side of the garden.'

'Always me…my…who do you think you are?'

The Large Grey Babblers, also called the seven sisters, are the only birds I know that can eat and argue at the same time reminding me of many noisy family dinners in my parents' home. Bengalis are famed all over India for their delicious cuisine but very few people know of their expertise at dinner table debates. Dinner at home always ended in an argument and the topics ranged across food, politics, marriage, children, Tagore, cricket and cinema.

The conversation usually started quite amicably with everyone commenting on the food, but after a few mouthfuls an aunt would remark that there was too much oil in the mustard fish. My mother would immediately reply that this was the way my great grandmother always cooked it.

'What is mustard fish without a generous sprinkling of raw mustard oil?' my father would say trying to pour oil on turbulent waters.

'You can put a little oil but not pour in a whole canister

to drown the fish,' the aunt would mutter, not willing to back down. She would continue to eat the fish curry though.

'You have a problem with everything I do or say. You do not like Uttam Kumar's films, you say my dogs are not well behaved, my sofa is too old.'

'The sofa is fine but the dogs are a bit spoilt, Ma,' this from my sister.

'Yes, you cannot sit on that chair because Prince Dodo does not like it,' my brother would mumble.

'Our dog has a sensitive nature. He is a highly pedigreed Lhasa Apso,' I would say, defending our evil-tempered dog who had bitten everyone in the family once and visitors twice.

'You keep quiet,' my aunt would scold. 'Always interrupting when adults talk about important matters.'

I was forty years old then but to my aunt I was always a brat with bad manners just like our beloved apso Dodo.

The acrimonious Large Grey Babblers must be carrying on like this except they do not sit around a dining table but rummage through the dead leaves instead.

It is odd that the seven sisters are called satbhai, or seven brothers in Hindi. I am sure the birds will have a lot to say on this matter too. The incessant chatter of the Large Grey Babblers is nothing compared to the relentless questions my six-year-old grandson, Shivam, attacks me with when we are out in the garden. It is a mild sunny day and the flowers are surrounded by winged insects. Beetles and grasshoppers are busy doing their thing in the grass under our feet. I am always eager to conduct nature study classes, so I make the mistake of pointing out a grasshopper to Shivam. 'Look at its long legs, see the wings, how green they are, just like the colour of grass so that no bird can find it when it is sitting in the grass.' As soon as I say this a myna swoops down and picks it up. It gives the startled grasshopper a quick bash on the head and begins crunching it noisily. The legs go first and then the green wings disappear into the myna's greedy mouth.

Shivam watches fascinated. After the myna flies away with a contented burp, the conversation, mostly one-sided, goes like this:

'Do birds feel hungry?'

'Yes.'

'What do they eat?'

'Seeds, sometimes insects.'

'Green grasshoppers?'

'Yes, sometimes.'

'Do the grasshoppers feel sad when the birds eat them?'

'Yes.'

'Why do the grasshoppers let the birds eat them?'

'They just do.'

'Why don't they run fast and escape?'

'I don't know, maybe they do try.'

A short pause and then:

'Who tells the bird to eat the grasshopper?'

I have no answer so Shivam thinks for a bit and says, 'Must be their mother who tells them.'

A pause and then he says to himself, 'His mother must have said, "You will get ice cream only after you eat the grasshopper."'

The sun is gradually getting hot now though you still find some cool and gentle days when the light falls in a delicate pattern on the trees, creating an illusion of a fine spring morning. The avenues of New Delhi are at their best now as the old trees drape clean fresh foliage on their heavy branches. You will see the tamarind tree standing, dark and handsome, serious and thoughtful, as it surveys the comings and goings in the old bungalows where most of our ministers live. This strong, sturdy tree was planted by the British on many main avenues of New Delhi. A wise choice since it provides shade in the summer and its heavy branches seem to absorb all the toxic fumes from the endless traffic on these roads. One of the oldest tamarind trees in Delhi is in the gardens of Humayun's Tomb. It must have seen many rulers, grand parades and turbulent days in its long life.

I often stand under a giant old tamarind tree on Teen Murti road and watch the Rose-ringed Parakeets as they nibble the tender leaves. The bird holds the green stem in its claw and eats the leaves delicately with its orange beak. The fern-like foliage allows the sunlight to filter through and the green of the parakeets merges beautifully with the leaves. The old trees have dark brown trunks with many nooks and crannies which make this tree a perfect nesting place for parakeets, woodpeckers and owls.

Monkeys too love to eat the tender leaves of the tamarind

but find the fruit too sour and spit it out with a grimace. The fruit, imli in Hindi, is much prized for its sour taste and is used in both north as well as south Indian cooking. From flavouring sambar and rasam to saunth chutney, the sour imli is loved by cooks all over India.

The fruit pulp is used to polish silver and brass and a glue made from the seeds is used as a fixative by miniature painters. A type of wild tamarind is found in the northeastern part of the country that has huge seeds. I have seen potters using this beautiful red seed to polish their unbaked earthernware pots to give it a glossy sheen when fired.

The city planners of Mughal India admired this tree and planted it along the major trunk routes. The name tamarind is said to be derived from the Persian words 'Tarmar-i-Hind' which means Indian date. A very sour date indeed but the fruit does get slightly sweeter when it is very ripe and soft. When the sour taste puckers your mouth remember the imli contains twice as much Vitamin C as an orange.

These last few days of spring are just perfect to explore the parks and old monuments of Delhi. Lodi Garden is my favourite place to walk in and I often drag many reluctant friends and relatives to show them the trees and birds in the gardens. 'I do not care,' said my young nephew when I pointed out a tree full of Green Pigeons to him many years ago on a cold winter morning. But then twenty years later I noticed he was pointing out that very tree to his young bride who looked suitably impressed. 'I did not know you were so knowledgeable about birds and trees,' she exclaimed and my nephew had the grace to blush.

Most members of my family are wary of coming for a walk with me to Lodi Garden. They find it embarrassing to stand under a tree and stare at nothing. Sometimes a crowd gathers around us as it always does in India if you stand still and look at something.

'You have a problem. May I help?' asks a kind gentleman as I stand gazing up at a ficus tree.

'Leave it, let's go,' says his wife.

'Have you lost something?' he asks again.

'No, thanks. Just some birds,' my daughter mutters.

'Ahh nature—we should all worship the goddess of nature, I tell you,' he exclaims, clapping his hands and scaring away all the munias I was watching.

'When I was posted as DC in Meerut in 1959, there was a stray cat… and a pigeon and…' he begins, eyes sparkling.

'The cat ate the pigeon. End of story,' says the wife as she drags him away before he can continue his tale; my daughter leads me away too in the other direction.

The ficus is loaded with berries all through spring and you will find at least twenty Green Pigeons feeding on this tree every morning. These plump birds with a friendly wide-eyed look, are not shy at all and allow you to stand quite close to them. Be careful though, or you may be showered with chewed up fig-berries or berry droppings. Called hariyal in Hindi, these birds are often shot by hunters in villages since they are said to be tasty. Despite this ruthless killing, the birds trust us and like to stay quite close to human habitations.

They have a soft, gentle cooing call unlike their aggressive cousins whom you can see all over the place.

This cooing of doves and pigeons is a favourite, familiar spring day's sound for me. Though it is still pleasant to sit outdoors or walk around in the park, there is a nagging, uncomfortable thought at the back of the head that the ***hot*** summer months are lurking just around the corner. I try not to think of them and enjoy the cool air as I walk down the shaded lanes of Lodi Garden. Ahead of me, a couple, obviously married for many years, is discussing the weather.

'It is quite nice and cool today,' says the wife.

'Not really,' her husband replies.

'Well, I think it is cool,' the wife insists with a shake of her head.

'I do not think so...see, I am sweating,' the husband says, wiping his brow in a dramatic gesture.

'You never agree with what I say,' hisses the wife.

'Is the weather my fault? I know, I know everything is my fault,' the husband says throwing up his hands in the air.

'I am never coming to Lodi Garden with you…you are really…' says the wife in a low whisper.

I could not hear the rest of the conversation since she had turned around and walked away. The husband carried on happily, whistling a merry tune under his breath. A little later I saw him walking with two other men, loudly discussing the weather once more. I was sure I heard him say how cool and pleasant it was. There was no sign of the wife. They could teach the babblers a thing or two.

Lodi Garden is probably the most popular park in Delhi. One can find almost every tree of northern India in this beautifully laid out space. On Sundays and holidays, people gather here in large groups as soon as the park opens. They are here for picnics, prayer meetings, family gatherings and yoga classes. There are serious joggers running down the lanes; they pass each other with a curt nod, never stopping to say 'Hello'. Important government officials walk here early in the morning and so do pretty young girls in designer track suits. Later, pairs of plump ladies arrive to chat and walk their calories away. At any time of the day you will hear interesting snatches of conversation on a variety of topics.

'My mother-in-law gave the diamonds to her…I was so shocked...'

'I told the deputy secretary clearly I will not tolerate this…'

'He said I looked really hot but then he turned around and said the same thing to her…imagine.'

'She caught her ayah sitting on the sofa with the cook.'

'You must add a little fresh mustard oil, only a little.'

The sprawling garden is laid out around the elegant tombs of the Lodi and Sayyid sultans who ruled north India during the fifteenth century. Once there was a village here and older residents of Delhi remember a dusty road running close to the tombs. The garden, then called Lady Willingdon Park, was laid out in 1936 with beautiful lawns and flowering trees. Many of the old trees were allowed to remain and they stand around the handsome Bara Gumbad and Masjid with the arched entrances, intricate patterns of calligraphy and the Sheesh Gumbad, decorated with tiles in two shades of blue of which only a few remain.

Fortunately the garden has not been 'beautified' by the horticulture department and there are many wild nooks and corners where you can see birds and butterflies on a good day. I have seen Scarlet Minivets, here flitting about the neem trees, but that was many years ago, before the mynas occupied prime territory in this garden. Scarlet Minivets are fairly common in the hills where the male flies about restlessly showing off his brilliant scarlet feathers while the equally lovely yellow female watches him indulgently.

On a fine day you can see the White Wagtail strutting about on the lawns, wagging its tail to let you know why it is called a wagtail. Though the first time I showed this bird to my young son, Siddarth, he was very upset and said,

'I thought you dragged me all the way here to show me a puppy but it is a silly bird again,' he sulked. He became very wary after that about going anywhere with me. 'What's the catch?' he would ask suspiciously and still does after thirty years.

I learnt very late in life that if you want children to learn about nature you have to do it very carefully, step by step, one tree, one bird at a time, otherwise they will grow up to dislike birds and trees.

Once I was, as usual, overdoing the nature lecture bit to a group, and I found that the children had hidden themselves behind a tree to escape from me. I quickly found them and then could not resist showing them the intricate pattern on the bark.

I tried the other day to show a sparrow to my four-year-old grandson Prithvi, a serious, thoughtful boy.

'Look there is a sparrow,' I pointed eagerly.

'How do you know it is a sparrow?' he asked.

'Well... it is,' I replied.

'Did you ask it, what is your name and it said my name is sparrow?' questioned Prithvi like an ace lawyer.

Since I had no answer, I kept quiet.

The crowds of happy picnickers ignore the wagtail though it is hovering quite close to them, most probably fascinated by the giant tiffin carriers. The group has brought enough food for an army and I can see a few of the women unpacking snacks already though they are yet to sit down.

My mother was very fond of picnics though not

necessarily outdoors. Our cook would prepare a mountain of parathas, alu subzi, kababs, ghugni—a delicious Bengali hot and spicy lentil dish eaten with puris—and various sweets. The food would be packed at night so that we could leave early in the morning for our chosen picnic spot which was always the Qutub Minar, for some reason. My mother had once heard in her childhood that someone had seen a tiger there and fifty years later she still believed that the animal was lurking around the tall minaret and the dangerous possibility appealed to her sense of adventure.

We all went to sleep early the night before and were warned that we must be up and ready by 6 a.m. sharp. Then when it was time to wake up, my mother would wave lazily from her bed and say, 'Looks like rain, better stay at home.' We would all go back to sleep for another two hours. When we woke up, we'd spread out the picnic fare in the veranda and eat our way through it steadily, occasionally glancing up at the clear blue sky.

Sometimes, she would actually take us for a picnic but then the cook would take a stove along and the food would be cooked 'in situ'. Once we travelled all the way to Siriskar which was a wild, lonely forest those days. We were accompanied by a reluctant cook who had been refused leave to go home for his nephew's wedding. He and my mother argued all the way and then just as we sat down under the shade of an old peepal tree, spread out our pillows, card games, plates, cutlery, tablecloth, books, fly swatters, hats, umbrella and other vital picnic things, our cook suddenly pulled out a knife and we all froze. Our mother continued to read her book.

'I will kill myself here and now if I cannot go to the wedding,' he said, his eyes blazing with anger.

'Put that butter knife down and start making the puris,' said my mother, not looking up from her book. The cook looked around sheepishly, then put the butter knife down and began rolling out the puris, whistling a cheerful tune under his breath.

On the way back the cook, whose name was Shankar, began telling us stories about the wild animals he had seen in his village near Rajgarh in Madhya Pradesh.

'We never went out after sunset because a leopard was always waiting right outside our courtyard wall. If we had to do our business urgently there was a big pot in the courtyard,' he recounted. 'My sister saw a wild dog dragging our goat away and she tried to chase it but the leopard came out suddenly and pounced on the dog. But soon six more dogs came out of nowhere and the leopard ran away. Leopards are scared of wild dogs who are not afraid of any animal. Luckily my sister managed to save the goat. This same sister's son is getting married,' he added with a loud sigh.

My parents did grant him leave later and my mother gave the bride-to-be a beautiful red silk saree, but we learnt later that Shankar's sister locked up the gift in the cupboard saying it was too good for her daughter-in-law.

The wild dogs which Shankar's sister saw are called dhole and were once found on the outskirts of Delhi, in the dry scrub and rocky areas towards Rajasthan. They hunt in huge packs and are considered more dangerous than leopards.

Kipling describes the hunting prowess of the dhole in *The Jungle Book*:

> What Won-tolla had said meant that the Dhole, the red-hunting dog of the Dekkan, was moving to kill, and the Pack knew well that even the tiger will surrender a new kill to the Dhole. They drive straight through the Jungle, and what they meet they pull down and tear to pieces. Though they are not as big nor half as cunning as the wolf, they are very strong and numerous. They do not call themselves a pack till they are a hundred strong; whereas forty wolves make a fair pack.

During these pleasant carefree days of spring when we try to be outdoors as much as possible, one of the familiar sights in all parks and open grounds where there is a water body is a long-tailed bird running up and down in an agitated manner. This is the wagtail, whom we have already met briefly. There are many kinds of wagtails here and all of them love open fields or well-watered lawns where they can pace up and down. These friendly black and white birds breed in the Himalayas and come to spend the winter in Delhi. They stay till late spring. It is very difficult to tell the various cousins apart unless they come up to you and introduce themselves in the true Delhi manner, for example, 'Myself Motacilla alba or Motacilla personata.'

They also have a close relative called the Yellow Wagtail

which is much prettier but a bit snooty since I have never seen it chatting to its poor relatives the White Wagtails. Another relative, the larger black and white bird called the Large Pied Wagtail lives with us throughout the year mostly hanging around water bodies and rivers. Since it is often seen near dhobi ghats where washermen work, the Hindi name for this elegant bird is dhoban.

Lodi Garden has hundreds of Rose-ringed Parakeets nesting in the broken walls of the monuments and one of the most wonderful sights is when a pair alights on the small square of brilliant turquoise still left on the tomb. A few hundred years ago the domes of these tombs must have been covered with these beautiful turquoise blue tiles and maybe the parakeets remember them from stories their ancestors told them and that is why they seem to cling to the tiny squares of brilliant blue.

There are three kinds of parakeet to be found in Delhi and each one as noisy as the other. The first and most common is the Rose-ringed Parakeet. Only males wear the chic pink neck scarf looking like Elizabethan dandies out for a stroll in the park. All they need is a silver-topped cane in their claws and a top hat. Hundreds of these birds can be seen flying over New Delhi at dawn and dusk as they commute from their home to their feeding grounds outside Delhi. These birds are often trapped and sold in the bird market despite it being illegal to keep them caged.

Some birds were taken to England as pets many years ago and now they have become permanent residents. I have seen parakeets screeching around in London parks or perched comfortably on old buildings, looking as if they have always lived here. They brighten up the dull grey skies with their brilliant green feathers though farmers and gardeners often complain that they damage their fruit crops. 'But they are so gorgeous that I do not mind sharing my strawberry patch with them,' says Ann, my English friend who has a small but beautiful garden in London with exotic plants such as green chillies, lemongrass and kiwis.

Another parakeet seen in Delhi is called the Plum-headed Parakeet. It is slightly smaller and the male has an elegant reddish head which he displays proudly at every given opportunity. I wish I could give him a tiny mirror so that he could admire himself at leisure. The female wears a sober but smart grey head and both always feed and chat amicably together despite their different headgear. This pretty bird is not easy to spot unless you are lucky enough to catch it on a fruit-laden tree, but is quite common in the hills where it loves to nibble on fresh peaches, apples and apricots. They have a low musical call which is very different from the other parakeets' high-pitched screeches.

The third and biggest parakeet seen in Delhi is the Alexandrine Parakeet. This bird with its powerful red beak and staring yellow eyes reminds me of my maths teacher in school who always chewed paan as he glared at me before striking through my sums with a red pencil. This parakeet does not screech as much as the other ones but startles you with a high-pitched call as if it has just discovered a murder victim lying on the floor.

Often, there are Spotted Owlets hiding on the branches of the jamun tree, waiting quietly for dusk to fall. Then they will glide out on silent wings to hunt for mice, lizards and other such delights. If you find a Spotted Owlet never look it in the eye. They seem to hate this and turn their head the other way around cutting you dead in no uncertain terms. If you insist on intruding on its space it will then bob its head up and down angrily before it flies off to a safer place. One of the most familiar owls, it is often seen on old trees with dense foliage where it hopes to rest during the day undisturbed by inquisitive people.

Once there was a pair nesting on a jacaranda tree in my garden and all our guests were given strict instructions (by me) to never look at them.

'All this nature study puts me off my beer,' complained one guest as he was forced to drink without raising his head. The birds did not mind the noise we made or the barking of the dogs, as long as we made no eye contact with them. They could look at us but we could not look at them—that was the rule.

The couple lived happily together, had several children and then their children grew up and moved into the same nest. Finally, after ten years, the old jacaranda tree died and the owls, now the third or fourth generation, moved away to a new address. They never came back to visit my old garden after all that I had done for them. There is no gratitude in the bird world.

The Black Redstart, on the other hand, is a friendly bird and does not mind if you stare at it for hours. This tiny, restless bird is a winter visitor and loves roaming our parks and gardens. The male is red and black while the female is a pale brown with an orange streak in its tail. They arrive from the Himalayas in Delhi by mid-October and stay till March enjoying the good weather and abundance of insects. The male and female never like feeding together and I have always seen them at opposite ends of my garden. But both have a habit of quivering their tail feathers in a restless manner very much like police constables behind a desk shaking their knees as they fill out an FIR. They are called thirthira in Hindi because of this restless twitching.

For years one bird, a female, arrived regularly around 14 October in my garden and stayed till end March never going anywhere all day. It stayed mostly in the shady part of the garden, picking up insects and then flying to a corner to eat them delicately like a well-mannered child. I have seen several pairs in Lodi Garden every winter, each one feeding quietly in its chosen area regardless of how crowded the park is. It has tiny black eyes which watch you as if the bird can read your mind and is trying to say friendly things to you.

While Lodi Garden offers a variety of trees, flowering shrubs and birds, another good place to find birds is the Sundar Nursery near Humayun's Tomb. You can wander here aimlessly and no one will bother you whether you buy any plants or not. In fact, when I did try to buy some seeds to take to my orchard in the hills where the planting schedule is different, this is what happened.

I walked into the room which clearly announced in large white letters on a blackboard 'Seeds for sale'.

'I would like some cauliflower seeds,' I said.

'Too late, come back next year,' said the fierce lady behind the counter.

'I need to plant them in the hills. It is still cold there.'

'Hills, ocean or fields…too late,' I said.

'You are too late for cauliflower, for spinach, for radish… too late for everything,' she repeated with a sigh and an irritated click sounding very much like my uncle who was a general.

'What about potatoes?' I asked. I had no wish to grow potatoes but it was becoming a matter of saving my honour now.

The other people at the sales counter looked at me with pity. They probably saw encounters like this every day.

'Come back next year,' they all said together.

I turned towards the door with a sad look at the seeds displayed in the cupboard. Cauliflower, spinach, carrots and potatoes—I could see them all stocked there. I had a sudden desire to snatch the packets and run for it but my courage failed me.

As a reward for my honesty, there was an Ashy Prinia singing outside the door as it hunted for insects on a hibiscus shrub. A long-tailed, tiny bird, it has a powerful voice and never stops singing, even for a moment, as it flits about. You will see it mostly on dried up grassy reeds; I was surprised to see it on the hibiscus. It had probably come to cheer up people retiring hurt from the encounter at the sales counter. I must add that the nursery has excellent plants for sale at very reasonable rates but you must be there at the right time.

The shaded flower beds, the long rows of seedlings and patches of open scrub are perfect places for birds and in one morning stroll through the nursery one may see Green Barbets, Coppersmiths, Flame-backed Woodpeckers, Red-vented Bulbuls, tailorbirds and maybe a lone White-throated Kingfisher. I have often seen a mongooses or two here going for a family outing or snake hunting. There are ruins of old buildings and stone walls where the mongoose like to hide; they come out when the coast is clear which is most of the time since the Sundar Nursery is a quiet, lovely place to wander about in except on 'Flower Show' day.

There are several rare trees here like the sandan, the empress tree and some so rare that nobody can tell me what they are and which you will never see anywhere else in Delhi.

The spring days flit by too quickly. Suddenly, one day the skies darken and there is a great cacophony outside my window. I assume it is the sparrows and mynas having a row over roosting space and look out to see is an amazing sight. Hundreds of Rosy Starlings are gliding in the sky. Like waves of black ribbons they circle and then settle down on the ficus tree, chattering like a hundred Delhi women at a kitty party before the food arrives. The entire tree is trembling with their chatter.

I was lucky enough one spring evening to see the amazing flight patterns these birds make as they get ready to leave. Ribbons of birds sway and dance in wide circles then gracefully swoop down low only to rise again in one choreographed movement. This stunning flying dance that the Rosy Starlings and other members of the starling family do is called murmuring.

These pink and brown birds come every winter to spend time in the fields and ponds around Delhi. I sometimes see them as they stop for a brief tea break on a mango tree outside my window before heading back to their nesting grounds in Central Asia.

The birds travel in huge groups and are said to damage crops wherever they go but they are also great locust eaters and can save a farmer's precious crop by finishing off all the locusts in one quick swoop.

They leave at dawn in great waves, flying gracefully as if just going for a joyride, quite confident about the long and dangerous journey ahead. They will return in August just when the rainy season is ending and if I am lucky, they may stop outside my window once more to rest.

The peepal is changing its colours every minute now and you may see one tree shimmering with tiny pale pink, rust and gold leaves while the one standing next to it may have glossy dark green leaves. It seems to enjoy putting out a gorgeous display of new leaves and one can see this hill of gleaming foliage only for a few days at the end of spring.

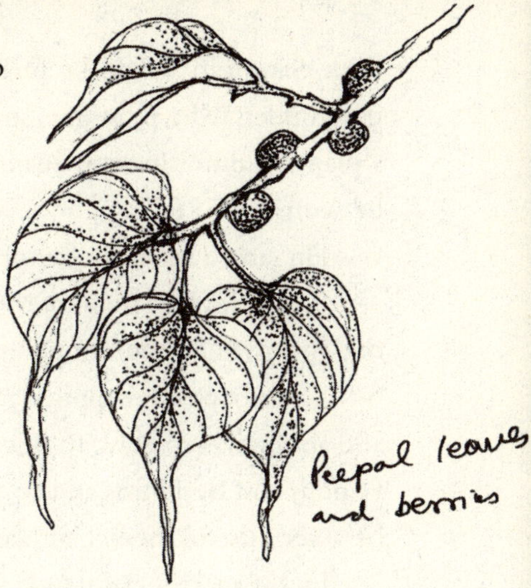

The peepal is sacred to Hindus and Buddhists and small shrines under old peepal trees is a common sight. In Buddhist sculpture, this tree are a symbol of Lord Buddha and in folktales, the peepal is the grand old tree of the forest along with the banyan.

The sacred tulsi starts slowly reviving in the warm light and every morning I see a few new leaves. This shrub is related to the basil family but has a more delicate flavour. The fresh green leaves are used as a herbal cure for coughs and colds, headaches, skin ailments and are very soothing for sore throats. The plant is grown all over India in decorative terracotta pots which are usually placed in the centre of a courtyard where it is watered at dawn. There are many legends about this plant, and here is my favourite one.

Tulsi lived happily in Vaikuntha, and her name was Vishnupriya, or beloved of Vishnu. But the goddess Saraswati was jealous of this name and often quarrelled with her. The delicate, sensitive Tulsi could not bear the insults and one day she vanished suddenly. Vishnu looked for her everywhere and finally found her hiding in a grove, heartbroken and sad. Vishnu, or Naryana, was now worried that if he brought her back, Saraswati would be furious and he was a bit afraid of the goddess's sharp tongue, so he decided to make Tulsi into a plant. And not just any plant but a sacred plant that would be worshipped forever.

He sang a hymn in her praise and said to her:

'My beloved, I shall forever hold you in my being and all the gods will honour you as a goddess.'

The story ends happily as Saraswati has a change of heart and apologizes to Tulsi. To this day the plant is worshipped by Hindus and Buddhists and considered by all herbalists to be a very useful medicinal plant.

In spring, the jacaranda looks up at the sky, checks the temperature of the sunlight and then suddenly brings out a bouquet of flowers. These delicate, pale mauve flowers are shaped like tiny tubes and change colour as they age. You may see them going from blue to pale mauve in one day if you have the time to stand under the tree all day. The ground below the jacaranda is always a carpet of mauve

since the flowers do not last long on the branches. I have never seen many birds on this tree except for a few Green Bee-eaters who hunt for insects amongst the half-open buds. They make a stunning combination of mauve and turquoise green as they perch on the branches.

By the end of March or first week of April, after the festival of Holi, the days begin to get warmer. But there is always a rude shock when winter gives us a passing sideswipe. Just when you feel summer has arrived and it is time to put away the warm clothes, the sky laughs and sends down a shower. The morning darkens, the afternoon brings out a pale sun and by evening you are shivering. You long for the sweater or shawl you just packed away in neem leaves. Spring is confused by this too and quickly sheds a vast quantity of flowers nervously. This sudden change does not last long and soon the cool weather packs up and leaves for good. Dust begins to rise in the rays of sunlight and spring finally leaves with a delicate wave of its hand.

From now till next year we will not see any migratory ducks, silk-cotton flowers, peanut-sellers, people lounging in the park or coral blossoms. The redstart and his wife head home, probably travelling separately and the lawns in Lodi Garden start looking bare as spring leaves. The English flowers have long disappeared. The parakeets still screech but just for fun as the garden no longer throngs with people who can hear them.

Now a sweet fragrance of jasmine will emerge at dusk and slowly the gulmohur tree will uncurl its green buds.

As the koel begins to call, summer will arrive in Delhi in a whirlwind of dust and settle down for a long, long time.

There will be endlessly long afternoons when all one can do is hide in some cool dark corner like a mole and read. Or doze. In offices people will try to stay indoors as much as possible and the parks will be strangely quiet at noon. The sun will be in its full glory, casting its powerful rays down, burning the earth, behaving like the powerful God it once was, worshipped by all ancient civilizations. Though we may no longer sing hymns in its praise, every living creature in nature knows the importance of sunlight and I believe, greets each morning with a silent prayer. We do, too, however hot and bothered we may be feeling.

SUMMER

The thirsty earth, parched and dry, scarred by the summer sun,
looks at the clouds all day,
Just as the chukor looks at the moon all night,
longing for love.

~HIMACHALI FOLK SONG

The sky is on fire, an eerie silence prevails and then the wind, stinging hot and cruel, blows the dry leaves and dust into a circle of frenzy. 'This is a witch dancing her magic dance to trap innocent travellers who make the mistake of coming to Delhi in June. This is the famous Delhi "loo".'

I hear my mother's words in my head as I watch the dry leaves spiral up in a vertical line. The mini-tornedo does appear a bit witch-like to me but I can see no helpless visitors trapped in it. In fact most people walk past ignoring this display of a temper tantrum by the summer wind and only a few crows are impressed by its force and fly around cawing with awe.

Every day the sun seems to get more angry as it looks down on us and I feel it is trying to engage the earth, or at least Delhi, in some kind of battle. From the moment it rises it blazes away, burning everything in its path. Sometimes the air you breathe is so hot you feel your lungs will burst into flames. The sun marches across the sky from dawn to dusk like a soldier waging war and everyone tries their best to keep out of its way. Birds stay in the cool shade of the trees, insects bury themselves in soothing tunnels of mud and we all try to stay indoors. It is only the trees who bask in this fierce sunlight and laugh with joy as the days get hotter.

The fierce summer sun brings out the most flamboyant and brightly coloured flowers of the year. The star flowering tree is the gulmohur with its spectacular display of blossoms. As soon as the summer sun takes centre stage in the sky to blaze down on us, the gulmohur begins its glorious display. Each flower has five delicate spoon-shaped petals and together they paint the tree in vivid tones of orange, red and scarlet—the colours an Indian bride wears. The pale green buds grow in clusters with silky red petals peering out of the green sepals. Parakeets love to nibble on these buds and while most people and birds are seeking shelter from the afternoon sun, they swoop down on the gulmohur for a noisy, happy meal.

Squirrels get very excited as soon as the gulmohur brings out its first buds. Each one wants the best, freshest bud and they run up and down the tree trunk chasing each other, sometimes getting entangled in the foliage and then falling to the ground. Squirrels are like acrobats and know how to hit the ground without getting hurt. Once a squirrel has eaten a few buds it will go away to relax in a shady corner but then return as soon as it sees another squirrel on its branch. Squirrels have a discordant bird-like cry which sounds like a war cry to me. It can be heard during the afternoons just when everyone is trying to sleep. Its untidy nest can be found right on the top-most branch of a tree from where it races down at top speed, screeching like a rowdy boy on a bike. To keep up their energy, squirrels nibble buds all day long. Yet the gulmohur still manages to produce enough buds which will flower and cover the tree like an orange-red shawl.

The light feathery foliage sways in the dusty, hot wind and sometimes a small Coppersmith may be found lurking in the green shadows. The tuk-tuk bird also wears the same green shade and a matching red cap like the tree. But it cannot bear to keep silent and can be heard calling out its monotonous song all through the hot summer day.

Strangely, the trio of birds which love to sing in summer, the koel, Coppersmith and the Green Barbet, just cannot stop singing once they begin.

All through summer afternoons, when the house is asleep, when shadows stand still under trees and not a leaf flutters in the blazing heat, the trio will begin their concert. I shut my eyes and resign myself to listen to their songs. The koel's voice is the loudest and like a soprano with an attitude, it tries to dominate the others but the Coppersmith has a call that is persistent and relentless. It will thrash out the same note over and over again and look very pleased with itself as it does so. You cannot help admiring its pride in its own skill as you watch it bobbing its little red head up and down as it sings the only song it knows. The song has only three words—tuk-tuk-tuk. And this why the Bengali name for this bird is tuk-tuk.

The third member of this trio, the Green Barbet, is a relative of the Coppersmith but unfortunately lacks its cousin's good looks and is famous in the bird-world for its ugly beak, its comical whiskers and staring, round eyes. But when it comes to vocal power, this bird, which is no beauty queen, will always win. A long, loud call which goes up and down discordantly and then trails away is what it is best at and it will match the koel in stamina any day. Every resident of Delhi knows these bird calls though they may not know the birds who produce them as the birds are usually heard but not seen. Summer to me is the call of these three birds along with the gentle cooing of doves. None of them are great songsters, but they do carry the languid summer mood in their voices.

As I hear the trio's non-stop calls, I am reminded of a cousin of mine who will grab the mike at every family function be it a wedding, a birthday or a funeral, and sing till everyone has fallen asleep or fled for quieter zones. The only way to stop him is to cut off the power supply. I am told every family has a compulsive singer tucked in its bosom, some great and others like our Coppersmith—non-stop, non-melodious performers.

In my family, apart from enthusiastic singers, we also have great talkers like the garrulous Coppersmith and sometimes one will help to smoothen out life's small hitches.

One hot summer's day I went to my bank along with my uncle who was visiting us from Kolkata. This relative, who was a senior officer in the police, had a commanding voice that could cut across huge fields and dales. We entered the bank and my uncle, after looking around disapprovingly at the way the bank officials were sitting around chatting and sipping cups of tea, said in his booming voice, 'Is there anybody free to attend to us?'

A lady who was talking on her mobile phone looked up with a frown.

'What is it?' she asked in an irritated voice.

'This lady here wants to cash a cheque, if it is not too much of a problem?' said my uncle in a voice which filled the entire bank and made the garlanded photo of the founder of the bank tremble.

The bank lady looked at him coldly and said, 'Yes, it is a problem. We are very busy today. The computers are not behaving.'

'I want to cash the cheque NOW,' he said again and thumped the desk, rattling the tea cups. Everyone was now staring at us. The guard at the door raised his gun nervously.

The bank lady, obviously a woman with nerves of steel, ignored us and resumed her conversation on her mobile phone, 'I have told you that I want the bathroom mirror at a correct height. You have fixed it too low. Am I a dwarf? How will I brush my teeth?' There was a brief pause as the carpenter said his piece.

'Listen, you will not get any more money from me. You have overcharged me in the first place for this mirror shelf,' the lady said, sipping her tea.

Again the carpenter said what he had to say. We could hear his voice now since, for some unknown reason, she had the mobile on speaker mode.

'You have paid me only half and till you pay the full

amount I will not fix anything.' And then for some reason he suddenly turned philosophical and said, 'Remember, madamji, we have come empty-handed into this world and will go away empty-handed. You give me Rs 300 otherwise I am not doing your work.'

My uncle, decorated for valour by the government of West Bengal, could not stand this anymore and snatched the phone from the bank lady.

'You will do as the madam says, you understand? Fix the mirror correctly at once. Fix it at the right height. Understand? That is an order,' he barked on the phone.

The entire bank had come to a standstill. I wanted to crawl under the cashier's table. But a strange thing happened. The bank lady put her phone down and stamped and signed my cheque. Within a few minutes the money was counted out to me by a grinning cashier as my uncle sat sipping tea with the bank lady.

I never went back to ask if the mirror was fixed correctly but my uncle was sure it was.

'Speak loudly and clearly to men, women, children and dogs and they will obey at once,' he said, reminding me of these lines from *Alice in Wonderland*:

Speak roughly to your little boy,
And beat him when he sneezes:
He only does it to annoy,
Because he knows it teases.

The hotter it gets, the more the gulmohur shows off its bright scarlet flowers and on particularly blazing days, the tree shimmers like a mirage of orange, green and gold on the horizon.

This ornamental tree has been planted all over Delhi and though it does look very beautiful in bloom, it is very delicate and has a tendency to topple over during heavy rainstorms. The gulmohur was brought to India from Mauritius but its original home is Madagascar where it once grew wild in the forests.

While the orange-vermilion gulmohur glows in the sun, a smaller tree brings out a display of frilly mauve, pink and lilac flowers to decorate its branches. Called the pride of India and also queen's flower though I am not sure which queen it honours—probably Queen Victoria—this medium-sized tree looks like a bouquet when it flowers. It stands proudly in most gardens and parks just asking to be admired. 'In full blossom in the morning the tree looks as if mantled with roses, but the flowers change through the day to a beautiful purple, making it appear at evenings, if seen from a short distance, like a bower of English lilacs.' Hunter wrote in description in great admiration and sheer homesickness.

The summer days stretch like a long empty road and you wonder when the sun will set and the burning earth cool down a bit. Sometimes the days are grey with a strange silver dust which makes everything around you look old and faded. You look out of the window on an empty street where even the stray dogs have found cool shade somewhere. Once summer is over and the days get shorter, I long for the lazy hot afternoons when you were forced to stay indoors. The languorous afternoons gave you time to read and think. Even those of us who had to go to an office somehow had more time to finish our work. The city slowed down, hiding in the shadows, as the sun burnt everything in its vision.

There is a wonderful legend about the sun which I tell my friends when the day is really hot and the electricity goes off.

The sun god Surya's wife was a beautiful woman named Sanjana, daughter of Viswakarma. She tried her best to be a good wife to him but soon found that she could not bear his fierce rays. She searched everywhere for a cool, shady place to hide but Surya's rays always found her. So she created a twin sister called Chhaya or shade, installed her in her own place, and ran away to the forest disguised as a mare. When the sun god discovered he was married not to the real Sanjana but to her shadow, he was furious, and disguised as a stallion, went in search of his true wife.

When they were reunited, Viswakarma, to help his daughter, trimmed the sun god's edges with his heavenly drilling machine. Despite being the architect-engineer of the gods, Viswakarma could only trim a tiny sliver from the powerful sun god. Out of these trimmings were made Vishnu's disc, Shiva's trident and Kuber's Pushpaka vimana, a magical chariot.

As I tell my story, suddenly I hear a cheerful noise

outside my window. I raise the curtains and look out. The blazing sun hits my eyes, blinding me for a moment. In the shimmering afternoon heat, I see a group of birds bathing in a muddy pool. As I watch them, my eyes slowly getting used to the fierce sunlight, I discover there is a very strict code of conduct which governs the bathers at the squelchy pool. First the crows waddle in, shrugging their shoulders as if getting ready for a friendly bout. They dip in and then quickly come out shaking their muddy wings and tossing their coal-black heads. Now it is the turn of the mynas who have been waiting under the peepal tree impatiently, muttering under their breath. The bad-tempered birds jump into the pool of water now made even more muddy by the crows, screech a few rude words, then fly up in the air and dive down again in a flurry of mud and dust. They are quickly joined by a group of sparrows that good-naturedly step aside to give the mynas more room to bathe. The water in the pool is now the colour of dark coffee but that does not stop the new arrivals, the doves, from stepping in. They hesitate only for a moment, like Victorian ladies stepping into old-fashioned bathing machines, giggle and coo a bit, and then walk into the puddle.

Meanwhile the sparrows are having a lovely dust bath nearby which keeps their feathers tick-free. Each sparrow has a tiny hollow of dust, which it enjoys as much as you would enjoy an expensive spa treatment. As I watch the drama unfold, a pair of Rose-ringed Parakeets flies in. They do not want to bathe, maybe they are afraid to get their glossy green feathers dirty, but they take a sip or two of the muddy water and then fly away. The rest of the birds, refreshed after their bath, are hanging around the muddy pool, chatting and preening, but just as everyone is having a jolly good time, a stray dog runs through the pool and ruins the fun. As the birds fly away, the dog settles down in the pool, which only has a few inches of muddy water left but enough, it appears, to give it some respite from the heat. I pull the curtain aside to see the dog has shut its eyes and is now dozing with a contented smile on its face. The small pool of water, which made so many creatures happy, has disappeared into the parched earth.

Birds and animals often share space since they all know how difficult it is to survive, especially in the wild. Jim Corbett writes about this amicable sharing of quarters in his book *My India*:

> The felling of the forest disarranged the normal life of jungle folk and left me with the care of many waifs and orphans, all of whom have to share my small tent with me. It was when I was a bit crowded with two broods of partridges—one black and the other grey, four pea fowl chicks, two leverets (young hares) and two baby four-horned antelope—that Rex the python took up his quarters in my tent. I returned an hour after nightfall that day, and while I was feeding the four-footed inmates with milk I saw the lantern light glinting on something in a corner of the tent and on investigation found Rex

coiled up on the straw used as a bed by the baby antelope. A hurried count revealed that none of the young inmates of the tent were missing, so I left Rex in the corner he had selected. For two months thereafter Rex left the tent each day to bask in the sun, returning to his corner at sundown, and during the whole of that period he never harmed any of the young life he shared the tent with.

Any cool place is a haven in summer, however crowded or small it may be. As a child I spent many summer afternoons in a grove of litchi and mango trees near Dehradun. The shade in a mango orchard is green and moist, amazingly soothing, unlike any shade you will ever know. A cool, wet-earth scented breeze drifts around the trees and though the sun is burning above your head, you stay safe under the magical green canopy where crickets are singing to burst their little hearts. The koel, of course, never stops calling while its mate, a shy but sly creature, hides in the dense foliage, occasionally screeching a reply. Another summer performer, the Green Barbet, relentlessly carries on its monologue with the world. I sometimes wonder if it is waiting for a reply from another barbet or each bird whether stating its own opinions like intellectuals in a seminar.

The mango grove shelters many birds not just in summer but in all seasons since the mango tree has something on offer all the time. In winter the bark is crawling with delicious insects which the Flame-backed Woodpecker loves to hammer out. In spring the branches are heavy with sprays of tiny scented flowers which attract insects and of course insect-eating birds like Bee-eaters, Paradise Flycatchers and Magpie Robins.

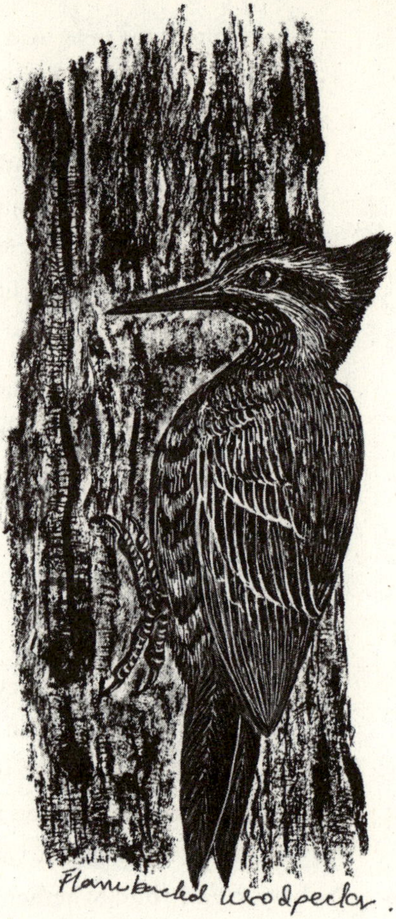

In summer, the mango tree is the best place for the birds to rest in to escape the afternoon sun and you will find a dormitory of snoozing Spotted Owlets, Brown Doves, Wood Pigeons and Red-vented Bulbuls. Once the tree is laden with fruit, the Rose-ringed Parakeets take over, shattering the peace of the long summer siesta as they feed; a heap of half-eaten fruits can be found lying all around the tree. As children my brother and I spent many hot afternoons aiming stones at half-ripe mangoes, competing with the parakeets to steal the best, juiciest fruits.

We were sure that a ghost lived in the dark green shadows and ate up all the sweetest fruits at night. There were always a circle of half-eaten mango seeds lying on the ground to prove our point. I know now that parakeets and monkeys were responsible for this and not some unfortunate wandering spirit with a fondness for sweet, delicious mangoes.

The mango tree has been cultivated in India for more than 4,000 years. It can be seen carved on the stupas of Sanchi which date back to 150 BC. The tree is sacred to Hindus because they believe that Shiva married Parvati under a mango tree. The leaves are used for every auspicious occasion and the wedding mandap is always festooned with fresh mango leaves. The mango blossoms which appear in spring are called the arrows of Kama, the god of love in Indian mythology. The great poet and playwright Kalidas wrote:

> They say the god of love
>   has flowers for darts
> And that the moon above
>   Is cold and chill:
> I am a wretch for whom
>   This works but ill.
> There is but little room
>   In lovers' hearts
> To bear such freezing rays
>   That burn and blaze
> Or to survive a flower
>   Of lightning power.

Legend has it that the mango tree came to India from Sri

Lanka. Hanuman, when he flew across the ocean in search of Sita, rested on a mango tree. He had a quick bite of the fruit and like most of us, found it delicious. He could not stop eating the fruit. Finally he threw the seeds into the sea and they floated back to India.

The tree flourishes outside Delhi but for some reason finds the soil here too dry; you may see many old trees but the fruit will never be as big or as sweet as those from neighbouring Uttar Pradesh. Maybe at one time the mango tree liked growing in Delhi. The area just past Mehrauli, called Andheria Mor, or the dark corner, had vast mango orchards. The evergreen mango trees cast such a dense shade even during sunlight hours that travellers were afraid to pass this place. I am sure many ghosts lurked here too, enjoying the cool, dark shade. Perhaps some are still wandering about in search of their lost mango grove.

Summer months in Delhi may be terrible during the day but at night you will be rewarded with the heady fragrance of raat ki rani, chameli and mogra flowers. The pretty white flowers are tiny but carry a powerful scent which many perfume makers have tried to copy. An old perfume shop in Daryaganj has a range of attar perfumes especially created for the summer months. The owner recalls how the wealthy gentry of the Old City used to saunter out in the evenings dressed in crisp white mulmul kurtas, a tiny swab of cotton-wool perfumed with summer attar, tucked behind one ear.

I tried doing the same but either my ears are the wrong shape or the cotton wool is not what it used to be because the swab I had drenched in rose attar fell into a mug of tea my husband was drinking, much to his horror.

'You smell like a cham-cham,' he declared, moving away to a safer, attar-free place to drink his freshly-brewed, unscented tea in peace.

Summer evenings in Delhi are languid with the scent of jasmine flowers erasing the day's hot and dusty flavour. Everyone who grew up in Delhi in the sixties will remember those summer nights when the entire family slept on the roof. A row of string beds, their white sheets gleaming in the moonlight, would be arranged according to seniority. My father slept in the best place, near the door, then my grandfather and grandmother on their hard wooden beds next to the earthenware surahi of water and two tumblers for their false teeth. A respectful distance away was my mother's place and then we children huddled close, beds almost touching. We whispered late into the night as the elders snored gently and the stars gleamed above to make us feel safe and loved. Sometimes I would see an owl gliding past, high above our beds, hooting softly as if trying not to wake us up. As the sky turned darker and the moon rose higher, I could see silhouettes of fruit-bats gliding low over the roof. They looked like messengers flying out to do errands for some wicked witch.

These harmless creatures live mostly on a fruit diet but have always been seen as something evil by humans. Some people believe they will attack you by wrapping their wings around your face. Bats have an uncanny sense of direction and will never crash into you however close they come. I have often pointed out to people a colony of fruit-bats hanging upside down during the day in their usual acrobatic manner on old arjun and jamun trees on Janpath but no one wants to know more about these endearingly ugly creatures who only love fruit.

As a child I would shut my eyes in fear when the fruit-bats came out at night since I thought they were going to attack me. I sometimes hummed a tune which I was sure would scare the bats away. My sister, sleeping in the next bed, once woke up and began muttering about too many mosquitoes buzzing in her ears. Soon everyone was awake searching for the elusive mosquitoes and I lay very still. Fortunately, a few mosquitoes who were minding their own business were found and quickly slaughtered and we all went back to sleep, much to my relief.

The raat ki rani filled the air with its sweet and spicy perfume and sometimes I would catch a shooting star racing across the sky. The sheets felt cool against my skin and the pillow soft as silk as I finally drifted off to sleep, dreaming of bats, mosquitoes and stars.

With a sudden shock the buzzing of the flies would wake me up rudely at dawn. As the sun rose, the perfume of the night flowers disappeared swiftly and one by one we gathered up our sheets and pillows and tottered downstairs to seek a room with a fan where we could snatch some sleep for a few hours more.

My mother always spoke with nostalgia about summer

afternoon siestas in a darkened room with khus-khus chatais on the windows. The hot dusty winds called loo would rattle the window panes but we would sleep on regardless. The youngest member of the family—somehow it was always me—had to get up every two hours to throw water on the khus-khus and a damp, sweet scent would fill the room. When I think back, it always seemed that summer days were longer when I was a child and we had endless time to read, slumber or just do nothing at all.

Not everybody has such nostalgic memories of summer days and nights as is evident in this letter an English civil servant wrote to his brother in England in 1833:

> The days are hot but the nights worse. I sleep outdoors under a mosquito net but the heat is terrible till very late. Then just when it gets a little cool and you finally drift off to sleep, the sun suddenly wakes you up with a knock on your head. I do not know how I will live through five months of this.

The older residents of Delhi still believe in natural ways to keep cool when the cruel loo blows. The most popular remedy to prevent heat stroke is to drink mango panna—a cooling drink made with the pulp of roasted green mangoes. The round, hard, football-like fruit, bael, is also made into a delicious sherbet. The pulp of the fruit has to be strained and sieved but the end result is always worth the trouble. The bael is one of the most sacred trees of India and is always planted outside temples dedicated to Shiva. It stands tall and green, its leaves rustling in the hot wind in old parks like the Buddha Jayanti Park as well as in many temple gardens of Delhi.

Summer in Delhi also means escaping to the hills—something we learnt from the British. The Mughals too moved their court to Srinagar during these months but it was only the royals who travelled to cool and green Kashmir to flee from the hot summer of the plains. The British moved to the various hill-stations like Simla, Mussourie, Ooty and Nainital.

'We moved in great style,' said an old English lady who grew up in India in the 1940s. 'Around mid-April, my mother began packing and then we children, our dogs, servants and guards all went up to Simla in one great flock. Our father stayed back and came up later when the Viceroy moved up. It was an amazing time for us. One day we were boiling in the fierce heat and the next day we were playing hide and seek on a cool, green lawn shaded by giant deodar trees. I remember my prickly heat always vanished at once.'

As the days get hotter, the gulmohur blazes on and the Green Barbet calls all day I long to be in the hills. I shut my eyes during the summer afternoons and dream about the green hillsides of Kasauli where the pine trees are scenting the air and wild flowers are raising their heads in every corner.

Kasauli, the nearest 'hill station' to Delhi is a quiet place, which has retained its old-fashioned values and I love to escape to its soothing emerald green shade during the fierce summer months.

During the days of the Raj, Simla was the summer capital of the British government, and though there were other hill stations this is where the 'posh' English used to gather. There are countless tales about how recklessly the memsahibs behaved once they were settled in the cool, salubrious climate of the hills. Kipling wrote many witty tales about the exploits of the ruling class in Simla as they rode and played around the hills.

Long before Kipling, Emily Eden visited Simla in 1839 and left a very witty, though sometimes a bit nasty, account of her travels in the book *Up the Country*. She writes about her journey to Simla in a hill dhoolie:

> It makes all one's bones ache to be jolted in a rough sedan for eight hours. The second day it poured till we came within sight of Simla, and with the sharp east wind from the mountains, the misery of all the dripping Bengali servants was inconceivable.

She enjoyed the mountain air and loved her 'jewel of a little house' and the hectic social life of Simla:

> We dined at six, then had fireworks, and coffee, and they all danced till twelve. It was the most beautiful evening; such a moon, and the mountains looked so soft and grave, after all the fireworks and glare.

Emily Eden was one of the few writers of her time to remark

on what the local people thought of all this gaiety, and wrote these famous lines in 1839 after the Queen's ball:

> ...and all this in the face of those high hills, some of which have remained untrodden since creation, and we, 105 Europeans, being surrounded by at least 3,000 mountaineers, who, wrapped up in their hill blankets, looked on at what we call our polite amusements, and bowed to the ground if a European came near them. I sometime wonder they do not cut all our heads off, and say nothing more about it.

Kasauli was never considered as fashionable as Simla by the British smart set. However, it still retains its quiet, old world charms because it is an army cantonment with strict rules about building or expanding. Old deodars shade the Upper Mall and you can walk around the town admiring many elegant, red-roofed houses with beautiful, tree-shaded gardens.

Kasauli's signature bird is the pretty little Red-billed Leiothrix also known affectionately as the pekin robin. The male is very proud of his olive green, bright yellow and red feathers and he will fluff out his chest and burst into song as soon as he knows someone is watching. The bird has a melodious call which rings out all over the hillside but you have to be very patient to actually spot the little bird. It flits about restlessly amongst the foliage and only sits if it finds an interesting insect. The male bird may give you an audience when he is in a romantic mood and singing a love song to his beloved. He puffs out his little chest and sings away, reminding me of Elvis Presley in his heyday.

As you walk around the paths of Kasauli, you will hear the Great Himalayan Barbet calling out in a monotonous voice. A not very handsome green bird with a grey-black head and clumsy yellow beak, the barbet likes the sound of its own voice very much and has plenty to say all day long. Sometimes its better-looking and more colourful cousin, the Blue-throated Barbet, will join in the conversation but each bird loves to talk endlessly and does not like to listen like many people we know. I feel if there is ever an election for birds the Great Himalyan Barbet would win hands down.

The fern-covered paths of Kasauli which meander along the hillside are where the Whistling Thrush likes to relax. This friendly bird will hop by your side, occasionally treating you to a low, sweet tune but it saves its best performance for early mornings and greets the dawn with a beautiful, melodious song. The bird is very well behaved and never intrudes on other birds' territory. It looks almost black in the shade but once it flies out into the sunlight you will see its gorgeous purple black feathers decorated with tiny shimmering dots.

A flock of Scarlet Minivets will suddenly flash by, their bright orange-scarlet feathers like a streak of colour in the sky. They often flit about on the pine trees, searching for insects. The male is a beautiful orange-scarlet while the female is understated but elegant in grey and yellow. Sometimes you may meet 'a mixed hunting party' which includes Red-headed Tits, Green-backed Tits, Grey-headed Flycatchers and several kinds of Willow-warblers including the aptly named chiff-chaff. These birds love to hang out together like old school friends, hunting for insects or just chatting. They are all tiny birds and all flit about restlessly amongst the foliage, never staying still even for a moment. They are as agile as acrobats and can hang upside down on the most delicate twig or twist about on a flower in search of a fleeing insect. They seem to love hunting at any time of the day and often catch an insect on the wing just to prove to their friends that they can do it better than them. Be careful when you try to follow this hunting party. I rolled down a steep khud chasing them once and had to be rescued by a group of school-children out picking wild raspberries. 'At your advanced age, you should be careful,' said a little boy as he pulled me up the rocky slope.

As the mixed hunting party flits about there is another member of the group that follows its own path. The Velvet-fronted Nuthatch likes to run up and down the tree trunk of a tall pine or a deodar looking for insects. I saw a beautiful nuthatch once in Khushwant Singh's garden and he said the bird was a regular visitor. I am sure he is watching the bird life in his garden from wherever he is.

In my orchard, a few hours away from Kasauli in a small village called Shaya, the birds will happily sit by your side since there is plenty to eat now though sometimes thoughts of mating make them go all coy and secretive. There is a Whistling Thrush that lives under my window and has appointed itself as my morning alarm. It starts singing long before the sun has risen behind the mountains and wakes up the dogs who begin to bark angrily at once, disturbing the cows who in turn let out bad-tempered moos. This opera is performed at dawn as the sky paints itself in pink and gold and the dragonflies begin to dance to the Whistling Thrush's melodious tune.

Gradually the hillside wakes up as Red-billed Blue Magpies screech with joy to greet the new day, flashing their brilliant blue and black feathers. These hill birds with long, trailing tails are expert thieves and each season manage to steal the maximum amount of fruit from the orchard. I have sat and counted with bitterness in my heart as a pair of magpies stole our precious plums one by one. In half an hour they had taken twenty-nine juicy, red plums meant for my table. They must have had a party planned in their nest because I heard them calling out gleefully to each other a few hours later.

The villagers consider this gorgeous thieving bird a pest and often shoot at it with homemade guns which misfire much to the bird's delight. It takes great pleasure in mimicking all sounds and one of its favourite is to mimic the mating calls of the Common Hill Partridges. It will settle where love-sick partridges are chasing each other around a tree and begin to sing in sweet notes creating confusion, misunderstanding and sometimes bitter heartbreak amongst the partridge gangs.

As the sunlight gets stronger Scarlet Minivets come out to play and catch insects on the pine trees. A sudden movement on the long tree trunk means the Himalayan Tree-Creeper is here too, looking for insects by creeping up and down the pine tree. That is how it gets its name in case you have not guessed it. Sometimes a pretty Velvet-Fronted Nuthatch may share the same space but the birds never bump into each other since each one keeps to its own designated lane on the tree trunk unlike Delhi drivers.

Afternoons belong to the Great Himalayan Barbet. This secretive bird will call all day long from various tree tops and the sound, echoing all over the hillside, makes it seem there are several birds calling at once.

There are marked changes in the hillside every season and they never look the same from month to month. The barren grey-brown meadows suddenly turn green in summer and hundreds of wild flowers appear as if by magic. Primulas, daisies, anemones, violets and buttercups form patches of colour on the grassy hillsides while the musk roses drape themselves elegantly on the trees and shrubs.

High on the mountains you will see sudden splashes of bright crimson red. This is the rhododendron in bloom. About two hundred years ago many plant hunters took this flowering tree to England and now it flourishes in almost every English garden. Horticulturists have managed to create a range of shades like pink, purple, red and pale mauve from the original red flower.

Many village homes in the hills decorate their doorway with the rhododendron flowers which are considered sacred and, of course, many others make a delicious, heady, home brew from the sweet flowers. I have often seen Himalayan langurs sipping nectar from the buds; one of them got so tipsy that he (I assume it was a male) fell off the branch much to the raucous delight of the rest of his troop.

On the hillside the resident toon tree is bringing out its rust and pale pink leaves just to show that it is different from most other trees on the hillside. Occasionally, you will see a wild apricot laden with white flowers and then all along the hillside there will be hundreds of wild pear and the delicate blossoms of yellow jasmine. The pine trees look washed and clean as if they are returning from a holiday after the harsh winter months.

These conifers of the Himalayas are very particular about the height they grow at and you can tell how high you are on the mountains by just looking around at these trees.

We begin with the chir pine—a tall but not very handsome tree found at around two to three thousand feet. Then comes the better looking cousin the blue pine which grows happily till almost 10,000 feet casting its gentle blue-green shade on the hillside. Then, as you travel along, you will meet one of the best loved trees of the hills—the majestic deodar, a tree closely related to the famous cedar of Lebanon.

A paper read by the botanist Sir Edward Buck to the Simla Natural History Society in 1885 mentions an old deodar near Kotgarh that had a girth of twenty feet and was said to be 500 years old. In Kasauli there are a few ancient deodars watching over the houses while in the forests beyond Simla and Chail there are still acres of dark deodar forests stretching into the mountains.

The next conifer you will meet is the fragile looking spruce fir which reminds me of a sad Christmas tree shorn of all its ornaments. As you travel higher you meet the last conifer—the elegant silver fir which was described by the poet Virgil 'as the fairest ornament of the mountains'. He was, of course, talking about the silver firs of Italy and not the Himalayan forest, which he had probably never heard about.

The trees and wildflowers of the Simla hills were very carefully observed and extensively written about by British travellers and residents. They were very curious about every plant and there are some wonderful books on natural history dating from the last century. My favourite is *Flora Simlensis* by Sir Henry Collett who lived for five years in Simla in the 1890s and made detailed studies of every tree, shrub, plant and flower he saw as he walked around the hills.

Back in Delhi, summer days pass slowly, and the sun, not willing to leave the stage, shines with vigour, doing its best to burn every bit of vegetation to a uniform dull brown. But the gulmohur stands bravely on the roadside to cheer up the weary soul and soothe the eye.

Then one day when the heat is unbearable and the air full of dust, you will suddenly see the magical golden flowers of the amaltas, or the Indian laburnum streaming down the branches of the tree like a wave of gold. This tree, so ugly a while ago, has suddenly transformed itself into a glorious creature. A tiny pyramid of golden yellow flowers dazzles heat-weary eyes. The best place to see the flowering laburnum is Shantipath though there are many equally beautiful displays of blossoms in Nehru Park, Lodi Garden and Buddha Jayanti Park. The delicate flowers do not last long and fall to the ground in a melancholic, languid way. The tree then reverts to its former not-so attractive self. As the summer days pass, it becomes more and more ugly. Misshapen, long, brown fruit pods hang from every branch of the tree and when the hot dusty winds blow they rattle in a most menacing way. They may look like a witch's wand and give the tree its Hindi name bandar lathi, or monkey's stick. These fruit-pods are used extensively in Ayurvedic medicines and are said to be a very effective laxative. It sort of ruins the fairy tale-like beauty of the flowering amaltas to know the pretty flowers will soon turn into laxatives.

During summer afternoons when the heat is turning

Delhi's streets into a furnace and most people are indoors, the male Grey Hornbill flies around looking for food for his wife. This clumsy looking bird with a huge curved beak is a devoted husband. The Grey Hornbill, a purely Indian species, has a complicated lifestyle. The female lays her eggs in the hollow of a tree, usually peepal or banyan, and then sets about building a wall with her own droppings. She uses her heavy beak like a trowel to flatten the plaster and to seal the entrance to the hollow but she cleverly leaves a tiny crack open.

Now she is a self-made prisoner. The male searches around for the best berries and brings them back to his mate. Then he proceeds to feed her through the crack in the plaster. The female stays captive in this 'nest' till the eggs hatch though she takes great care to keep her home clean by throwing out rubbish through the tiny slit window. Then one fine sunny day in summer she breaks open the plaster and emerges into the fresh air. At first she looks a bit dazed by the sunlight but soon recovers her poise and the happy hornbill pair congratulate each other for successfully bringing into this world yet another brood.

I wonder if the Grey Hornbill fledglings ever acknowledge their mother's sacrifice to hatch them in such total security or do they like most teenagers say, 'What did you ever do for us?'

You will often see these birds gliding around Lodi Garden squealing in a curious way as if they were mimicking newborn kittens. The Grey Hornbills have a slow, ungainly way of flying from tree to tree in search of vegetarian fare or small insects and often rest on the highest branch to view their surroundings in a thoughtful manner. Once you have seen these endearingly ugly birds with long, dangly tails and movie starlet-like thick eyelashes, you will never forget them.

In summer, the garden wears a forlorn look with all the flowerbeds a jungle of dried weeds. The few plants in the flower-pots look tired and thirsty since we try to use the minimum amount of water for all the plants and I often feel like a prison warden as I dole out half a mug of water to each flower pot. 'We should let them all die because they will all come alive after the rains,' is my mali Jagannath's advice. He wants to go home to prepare his fields before the rainy season; also, yet another nephew is getting married. I often wonder if Jagannath's nephews keep getting divorced and remarried or whether he just has many nephews. He is still very upset about the death of his mother-in-law, who was apparently 100 years old. 'She was so healthy...ate six chappatis every day,' he keeps saying to me. His wife does not seem so grief-stricken. 'Imagine a man missing his 100-year-old mother-in-law so much…the fool. The old lady lived a good life and died happily,' she says as she helps me move the plants under the shade of the green neem. Jagannath is too sad and mournful to work today.

The next day I find a stray cat has given birth to a litter of five kittens in the green shade. The mother looks so harassed and thin that I do not have the heart to chase her away but the dogs are not happy about this intruder. Watering the flower-pots now becomes a dangerous and devious exercise. I have to sneak out through the back door with a bucket and mug, looking like a villager going for her morning ablutions, and water the plants in a furtive way. The mother cat watches me suspiciously but I have brought a small bottle of milk for her. She looks at me in that cold, ungrateful manner many cats have and then proceeds to lap it up as I smile at her in an ingratiating way, hoping to make friends. Meanwhile my dogs have sighted this treacherous act of mine through the window and are trying to break down the glass panes. I quickly water the flower-pots and leave.

One day, when the garden is shimmering in the oppressive heat, the mother cat leaves, taking her five kittens with her. No thank you and no good bye. I can see the dogs laughing at me with a 'We told you so' look in their eyes.

The greenest thing you can see now is an old banyan tree down the road from our house. Its aerial roots and dense foliage shelter many birds and the tree is always alive with bird calls. In Delhi, the tree does not grow to the great girth it can achieve elsewhere. One of the most beautiful banyan trees I have ever seen was in the Ranthambore National Park in Rajasthan. Standing under its vast green canopy, spread like a giant umbrella of leaves, I felt like a time-traveller who had travelled into a magical world of dancing leaves, flying roots and hundreds of singing birds.

The dry heat brings out the musical best in the Magpie Robin and it sings softly as it hunts for insects. This dapper black and white bird always looks like a smart lawyer just returning from court after winning a case. It whistles as it hops about and is so friendly that it will often come and perch on my chair if I sit still and will sometimes even taste a bit of leftover breakfast.

Whistler wrote in 1928 about the Magpie Robin:

> It is both confiding and unobtrusive, and as the lady of the house moves about the garden in the shade, whether she be burra-memsahib or some humble menial's wife, she will see the little pied bird watching her from wall or bush with friendly and attentive scrutiny. And by way of gratitude for shelter and protection (or so we like to think in spite of prosaic fact), the cock bird early in the morning and again in the evening mounts to the topmost bough of one of the garden trees and pours out his delicious song. For the Magpie Robin is one of the best songsters in a land where singing birds are somewhat scarce.

Despite all this heavy praise from Whistler, the humble Magpie Robin remains very down to earth probably because most people think it sings too much and too early. 'I will wring this bird's neck,' declared my son Siddarth when he was a teenager, as soon as I pointed out who was responsible for all the loud music at dawn. If the Magpie Robin was not such a kind creature I would think it was taking revenge for being made to stay awake till the late hours in the morning by my son's blaring heavy metal bands. My son, who is now thirty-six and a responsible father of three kids, denies all this.

Gradually summer days get more and more humid and

everyone begins to talk about the monsoon. When will it break over Kerala, will it arrive on time in Delhi, will it be strong or weak?

Every home in India is affected in some way by the great monsoon and everyone has a theory about it. From poets of ancient India to present day economists, from farmers to housewives, we all like to think we know this amazing phenomenon better than others.

Meanwhile the skies darken but there is no sign of rain. Drenched in sweat we look towards the heavens but nothing is happening. Then I hear a strange, squeaking sound as if someone was trying to open a rusty old door. My heart jumps with joy because I know it is the Pied-Crested Cuckoo—the harbinger of the monsoon. This handsome black and white bird has a smart crest on its head and appears to be dressed for a formal dinner. Rumour has it that this lovely bird comes to us all the way from Africa, riding on the monsoon winds but this theory, which is so romantic, has yet to be confirmed by ornithologists.

I have seen it for the last ten years regularly during the last week of June though once in 1983 I saw a pair sitting cozily together on the jacaranda tree in my garden in July. Maybe this pair had eloped and stayed back to enjoy their honeymoon in Delhi. The Pied-Crested Cuckoo, like its cousin the koel, is parasitic and does not believe in nest building. It lays a beautiful sky-blue egg in the nest of the babblers and laughing thrushes. The young Pied-Crested Cuckoo ejects the rightful offspring from the nest and then flies away to sing its shrill song.

Every June I wait impatiently to see this elegant black and white bird, hoping to hear its squeaking notes which Dr Salim Ali wittily compared to an unoiled bicycle. Then suddenly one morning our monsoon herald is here, perched on the topmost branch of the jamun tree, calling out in its unmusical voice. 'It will rain soon,' I announce smugly to my family. 'The Pied-Crested Cuckoo has arrived.' They look at each other and shrug in that disbelieving manner my family members have when confronted with my 'yet-another-nature-study' remark. The only person who was always as excited as me about the arrival of the Pied-Crested Cuckoo was Khushwant Singh. He always wrote in his popular newspaper column about the monsoon bird's safe arrival in Delhi and was responsible for thousands of people actually learning about this amazing bird.

The next day it begins to rain. Not a downpour, just a gentle passing shower, enough to keep my faith in the Pied-Crested Cuckoo's announcement and rejoice. The family has no comment.

Summer is now packing up to leave and the parched parks and gardens of Delhi heave a sigh of relief. The roads will soon be flooded, the mosquitoes will flourish and the last flowers of the gulmohur will fall. Everyone is looking at the sky with hope. The clouds arrive, huddle together for a while and then suddenly disappear. The sky is a clear blue once more but the air is so humid that you can taste the moisture.

The brainfever bird now gets hysterical and you can hear

its triple note call being repeated endlessly as if calling for the rain. This bird calls all throughout summer but for some reason towards the end of the season it gets into a real frenzy. This shy, secretive bird is actually called the Common Hawk-Cuckoo but the English were so traumatized by its call during the 'hot season' they decided to give it this unflattering name. You will find it mentioned in many tales from the days of the Raj where it is always driving some poor, bored English memsahib around the bend with its incessant calls. The bird is mentioned rather unkindly in several works by Somerset Maugham when he talks about the ennui of the Englishman or woman living in some forsaken corner in the East.

The pre-monsoon showers begin on a quiet, listless note but Delhi is thrilled and children rush out to bathe in the first shower. I do too because my mother used to say it is the best cure for prickly heat and allowed us to bathe in the first shower. But it is a false rain and within minutes the sky clears and we stand around in the bright sunshine, looking damp and foolish.

Then suddenly a lone frog gives a faint croak to raise our hopes. This is a sad discordant farewell to yet another fierce summer and as the poet Amaru says:

> The summer sun, who robbed the pleasant nights,
> And plundered all the water of the rivers,
> And burned the earth, and scorched the forest trees
> Is now hiding; and the autumn clouds,
> Spread thick across the sky to track him down,

Hunt for the criminal with lightning flashes.

As we wait, scanning the skies for more clouds to come and rescue us from the cruel heat, the soil too waits for the rains. The scorched grass, the wild plants and many trees like the neem and jamun are getting all their seeds ready and as soon as the rains come they will send them down at once. Insects have laid thousands of eggs which will hatch as soon as the first showers come. Every creature is waiting anxiously for the monsoon and nowhere else in the world do you see this kind of expectation in men, women, birds, animals, plants and insects for the same thing—rain.

While Delhi waits for the monsoon to arrive as eagerly as a bride waits on her wedding day for her groom to arrive on a white horse, other cities of India like Kolkata, Chennai and Mumbai are already dealing with floods.

The narrow street in front of my grandmother's house in Kolkata would get flooded as soon as the rains arrived. The water would rise up quickly to touch the steps of the front room. Then it would continue to rise and soon we would be marooned in our house, unable to venture out at all.

We, who had newly arrived from dry, dusty Delhi, would stand at the window to watch the amazing sight of people being ferried across the street in tiny make-shift boats. A smart young man, worried about his pristine white shirt and pants, climbed on the shoulders of a burly fellow who effortlessly carried him to a safe, dry place. As we watched, he took out a crisp ten-rupee note to pay his carrier. The men would be ferried to their cars parked on the main road in their individual little boats which looked like giant saucers. The women and children stayed at home while the servants waded happily in the water to the market. They were pleased with the flooded streets because now they had a valid excuse to spend hours roaming in the market with their friends.

My grandmother, who stood tall and regal at four foot two inches, would be waiting for them at the door like a sergeant major, waving her walking stick. Dripping rain water all over the floor, the old cook would look my grandmother right in the eye and say, 'I fell into a gutter'. Though his shopping bag and all the vegetables and other groceries were dry, he always got away with this excuse. As he walked into the kitchen, my grandmother would frown and curse the rains.

'Why does your bundle of bidi always stay dry when you fall in the gutter?' she would ask but the cook would quickly disappear into the safety of his kitchen.

The rest of the day she would spend playing mournful tunes on the piano and making all of us recite poetry to her. My brother and I knew only a few Hindi and English poems and were treated with scorn by my highly accomplished Bengali cousins who could recite Tagore's poems and sing beautifully. They could also dance, play the sitar and paint with great skill and always made us feel inferior.

Every morning my grandmother fed the crows tiny balls of rice which she would make herself. She believed that if you fed crows regularly with your own hands, the gods would grant you a painless, swift death. She did get her wish and died peacefully at the age of ninety-eight surrounded by her children, grandchildren and great grandchildren. In my mother's recollection, a dozen crows gathered outside her window at dawn and sat quietly as if saying a silent goodbye to the old lady who had fed them for so many years.

When we came back to Delhi, just before school opened, the monsoon was well settled in Delhi but that romantic, melancholy air of Kolkata flooded in the rains, strains of Rabindrasangeet floating out from open windows, coconut palms drenched with raindrops, was missing.

In Rabindranath Tagore's *Gitanjali*, the poet's heart longs for the rains:

> The rain has held back for days and days, my God, in my arid heart. The horizon is fiercely naked—not the thinnest cover of a soft cloud, not the vaguest hint of a distant cool shower.
>
> Send thy angry storm, dark with death, if it is thy wish, and with lashes of lightning startle the sky from end to end.
>
> But call back, my lord, call back this pervading silent heat, still and keen and cruel, burning the heart with dire despair.
>
> Let the cloud of grace bend low from above like the tearful look of the mother on the day of the father's wrath.

MONSOON

In the deep shadows of the rainy July
with secret steps, thou walkest, silent
as night, eluding all watchers.
Today the morning has closed its eyes, heedless of the insistent calls of the
loud east wind, and a thick veil
has been drawn over the ever-wakeful blue sky.

~ *Gitanjali*, RABINDRANATH TAGORE

One day I wake up and there is a strange, damp scent in the air. The sky is still a clear blue but then in one corner I see something taking shape as if an unseen hand has been drawing circles with a charcoal stick. The next day more fluffy white and grey shapes arrive out of nowhere and take over the sky. The sun looks unhappy and sullen as it tries to push these intruders away but fails. Now dark silver-edged clouds play hide and seek all day as Delhi changes its mood to greet the rains. One day it is dry and dusty, then suddenly it gets hot and humid like a southern state where it is warm and wet all year round. Soon the parched fields will be lush with green foliage, erasing the memories of those arid, cruel days which made everyone hide indoors in darkened rooms.

There are peals of thunder every morning heralding the rains but nothing happens. We watch the sky, scan the newspapers to check where the monsoon has reached. 'Monsoon delayed' shout the headlines as we sweat it out in the north, envious of the happy, rain-drenched states where the monsoon is spending extra time.

Slowly and steadily, like a giant tortoise making its way uphill, the rain clouds, laden with moisture, make their way to us. We wait. We perspire. We grumble. There is a stillness in the air, as if every living creature was holding its breath, waiting for something to happen. The leaves barely move on the branches, the birds sit quietly and even the crows are strangely uncommunicative with each other.

Just when we have given up hope, the monsoon arrives like a mighty emperor riding in to conquer new lands. The skies darken; there is the roar of thunder and lightning races across the grey sky in a frenzy of broken silver lines. It is twilight at noon. We wait and watch, quivering with excitement. There's a brooding heavy silence, every blade of grass holds itself still, and then quietly it begins to rain. Shouting with joy I rush out, along with the children, to taste the first drops of rain. All around me people are laughing as they raise their faces to the sky. The rain makes a beautiful drumming sound all around us as the breeze, cool and scented with raindrops, races around the house.

The trees bow their heads to greet the rain and street dogs begin barking and chasing each other as if they had never seen rain before. Many of them were probably not born last year and are frightened of the downpour.

Within minutes the roads are flooded, the parks look like marshland and from nowhere, hundreds of frogs appear and begin to sing their discordant, mismatched songs. Everyone—people, trees, birds, plants and insects with millions of larvae waiting to hatch, are overjoyed that the monsoon has arrived. The parched thirsty land soaks in the water quickly but small pools begin to form by the end of the first day of the rains. As if a forest goddess has waved a magic wand, overnight every blade of grass turns a vivid shade of delicious green and every tree looks clean and sparkling.

The air is fragrant with the scent of fresh, green grass and mysterious wild flowers. The wet earth sends out a perfume which is uniquely Indian. It is called mitti and many perfumers from Mughal times onwards have tried their best to recreate this subtle, earthy scent in their attars but I feel they have not managed to catch the unique scent of that fleeting moment when rain falls for the first time on dry earth. You have to be present in Delhi on the first day of the monsoon to experience this incredible, unforgettable scent which will not appear again till next year.

Butterflies of pastel hues emerge to greet the rains and along with them come a host of other flying, biting and stinging insects. Bees hover over the flowers which have sprung up along the roads. There are many other bigger

and more colourful flowers in the park but the bees seem to like these tiny, nondescript flowers which one can hardly see unless you are a keen botanist, peering into every nook and corner.

I fall into a ditch trying to examine a tiny white flower and am chased by an irate stray cat who thinks I am trying to take over her safe home under the drain. She has five kittens, I notice, who are happily playing in the mud. A mongoose watches me suspiciously, nostrils quivering, as I walk down the muddy path. Now there is a triangle of suspicion as the cat, mongoose and I circle the ditch. The mongoose would like to catch a kitten, the cat would like to chase the mongoose and me away while I would like to just watch them and pick a few wild flowers. Only the kittens seem happy and carefree as they tumble around in the rain-drenched ditch.

All is resolved, though not amicably, as a pair of crows joins our discordant group to drink water from the ditch. The cat drags her kittens to a safer place deeper in the ditch, the mongoose disappears and I am left alone with the crows clutching a handful of white flowers crawling with red ants. I drop them quickly and walk away. I can hear the cat and the mongoose hiss, 'Serves you right, interfering human.'

I go and sit quietly on the veranda and watch the bees dance over each tiny flower in the garden in a most affectionate way, as if meeting a long-lost friend, and think of Kahlil Gibran's words:

> And now you ask in your heart, 'How shall we distinguish that which is good in pleasure from that which is not good?'
>
> Go to your fields and your gardens, and you shall learn that it is the pleasure of the bee to gather the honey of the flower,
>
> But it is also the pleasure of the flower to yield its honey to the bee.

This abundance of fresh, delicious, green vegetation and insect life is a glorious time for birds and many species very cleverly take advantage of this bounty to make sure their new brood has already hatched. The Black Drongo may nest in the rainy season and the Baya Weavers always do but the tiny White-eye is always worried that its fragile nest will be washed away in the rains. This little green-brown bird may come stare at you with anxious white-edged eyes as if asking for reassurance. It is not easy to see the bird when it hides in the dense foliage because its colouring matches the leaves perfectly but since it is a restless bird, it can be seen as it moves from branch to branch in search of insects.

Sparrows, mynas and parakeets gather in the muddy little pools that have formed all along the roads and a frog may be heard croaking in delight. But its joy is short-lived as this is just what the kite was waiting for. A few bashes on the head and it swallows the frog whole. The frog clan sets up a loud, sorrowful lament and the brainfever bird joins them at once with a high-pitched song which will go on for an hour.

But this is probably the last time this year one will hear its strident call.

One rainy afternoon, walking past a muddy puddle, I saw a strange sight. My footsteps had disturbed a plump mother frog and her eight babies. After glaring at me like only a frog with bulging eyes can, the mother gave a little nod. In a second all her babies rushed towards her. Now, to my amazement, each tiny frog jumped on its designated spot on its mother's body. As I watched, two leapt on her upper back, two jumped on her lower back while one flew straight up and landed on her head. The remaining two attached themselves to her front and back legs. Now the mother frog looked much bigger and bolder as she fixed me with an angry look which said, 'Get out of my space…or else…'

I was really impressed with this meticulously planned strategy to gather her babies and chase off predators in one move by making herself twice or thrice her usual size, although I did wonder how this strategy would work in there were an uneven number of babies.

The trees, feeling lighter now that the summer dust has been washed off them, bring out hundreds of new leaves, every leaf a different shade of green. The jamun is a glossy pale green, the jacaranda a slightly darker green and the peepal a glorious shining emerald. The mango wears a dark, mysterious green while the alstonia's seven leaflets are the palest of jade green. The ashok tree suddenly seems several inches taller with its gleaming crown of polished, deep-green leaves.

It does not rain every day and sometimes the sky is a clear blue but the moisture in the air is so heavy you can taste it. The monsoon sky is full of drama—a stage where the sets change every hour. One day I wake up to find the sky a clear blue with just a few stray wisps of innocent-looking white clouds. Within half an hour, more clouds arrive from some hiding place and chase the white ones away. Now the sky is a blanket of grey, rough clouds, each one fat as a pillow. It begins to rain, then stops as if someone has turned off a tap. The sun comes out from where it was waiting patiently in the wings, all ready to take this chance. It probably misses being the all-important star which dominated the stage just a few weeks ago and longs once more to be the golden god ruling over the skies and the land.

A grey, misty steam rises from the trees and Delhi turns into a sauna. An hour later, the sky changes again and dark clouds charge in. They take their places, standing in opposite corners, glowering at each other like rival football teams. More clouds float in, each one a strange shape as if going to a fancy dress party for clouds.

I can see an elephant, though my granddaughter Naina insists it looks like a rhino and then we see a cloud which looks uncannily like my favourite Hindi film star—Aamir Khan.

The sun retires hurt. While some lazy clouds like to hover in one corner of the sky, other more energetic ones begin to march heavily across like a herd of elephants. The light changes from pale grey to gold and then to a dark slate grey as the drama continues. Sometimes it is a light-hearted play with gentle rain and soft thunder or it is a great tragedy being played out with deafening claps of thunder and fierce lightning along with rain that is powerful enough to strike you down.

The most beautiful sight during the monsoon is the glorious sunset. As thunder beats out a melodious rhythm and lightning makes patterns across the sky, for a few magical moments the sky paints itself with brilliant streaks of orange, pink and gold.

The Pied-Crested Cuckoo has already announced the rainy season and now sits looking very pleased with itself as it calls out from the topmost branch of the peepal tree in case anyone has missed the fact that the rains have arrived in Delhi. I can hear it sing in a smug tone, 'I told you so… I told you so…'and I too echo its call but silently in my head since I do not want to sound too smug.

As we walk across the wet and muddy path which surrounds Humayun's Tomb, a gang of beautiful little Green Bee-eaters comes out to hunt. There is so much delicious stuff for the birds to eat now—termites, ants, beetles and crickets—that they cannot stop hunting even when their tiny stomachs are full. Like small green paper planes, the bee-eaters take off in the air, circle for a moment and then effortlessly catch their lunch on the wing. The rain does not seem to bother them at all and while we sweat and grumble, slapping the mosquitoes which are greedily attacking our arms, the insect-eating birds are out having a feast especially on days when the ants and termites swarm, proudly showing off their nuptial wings, unaware that they will only live for a day.

Strange creatures invades the house. One day I find a toad in the bathroom. It had obviously hopped in to use the 'facilities' as Victorian ladies used to say. We wait patiently for it to come out but it is taking as much time in the bathroom as my friend's teenage daughter. I see it cleaning its face with a special face wash, putting on all kinds of creams and then just standing there gazing at its reflection in the mirror.

An unusual hymn from the Rig Veda describes the rejuvenation of frogs when the rainy season arrives:

> When the heavenly waters came upon him dried out like a leather bag, lying in the pool, then the cries of the frogs joined in chorus like the lowing of cows and calves.
>
> As soon as the season of rains has come, and it rains upon them who are longing, thirsting for it, one approaches another who calls to him 'Akhkhala' as a son approaches his father.
>
> One of the two greets the other as they revel in the waters that burst forth, and the frog leaps about under the falling rain, the speckled mingling his voice with the green.
>
> When one of them repeats the speech of the other, as a pupil that of a teacher, every piece of them is in unison, as with fine voices who chant over the waters.
>
> One lows like a cow, one bleats like a goat; one is

> speckled, one is green. They have the same name but they differ in form, and as they speak they ornament their voices in many ways.

Every lane, ditch and garden is green with plants and if you walk around the Ridge you may even hear little hidden streams gurgling mysteriously. There are wild flowers in the corners and each one seems to have a resident snake on guard. A White-breasted Kingfisher sits on an electric pole, its blue wings hidden, pondering on the meaning of life and whether to catch a young frog or a grasshopper today. The smaller, brilliant-blue Common Kingfisher is not so commonly seen now and I miss its tiny blue figure hunched by the nullah near my house, its lovely turquoise blue feathers gleaming in the rain.

The rains would turn this nullah into a gushing stream teeming with a variety of insect and bird life. Silver-winged dragonflies would flit on the muddy waters chasing their potential mates but their courtship was often cut short by the kingfisher. My son Siddarth, a boy of eight then, always made sure he saw the blue kingfisher before he boarded the school bus and one day he refused to go to school because the kingfisher was not there to wave him goodbye. 'A very unusual excuse for missing school,' his teacher said in a stern voice the next day to me. Many years later she asked me to give a talk about birds to the school-children and told me not to mention the kingfisher episode 'since it would set a bad example to the students and encourage them to think up flimsy excuses when they came late to school.'

'Truth is always stranger than fiction,' I said to her but she was not impressed.

Tiny yellow, blue and white butterflies flew about aimlessly and were snapped up by the giant toad that had established residence by the nullah. He–I assume it was a male toad—looked and behaved just like an old mafia don and all the lesser beings in the nullah paid their protection dues to him and some unfortunates one were eaten during the unfair exchange.

One day, when the rain had made the ground wet and slippery, I saw a pair of Black-winged Stilts strolling on the grass but they did not stay for long once they realized that this was only a humble, muddy nullah and not a fast-flowing river or large pond they usually hang around in.

The big fat bully toad went into hiding when the stilts arrived and only reappeared looking a bit sheepish after the birds had flown away.

I was reminded of this story from the *Panchatantra* when I saw the Black-winged Stilts flying in the sky, their long red legs trailing behind them.

Once, a pair of geese decided to help their friend, an old tortoise, by taking him to a better feeding pond. They asked him to hold on to a stick with his mouth and the pair flew up into the sky, holding the stick between them. 'Do not open your mouth to speak,' they had warned him before they took off. People on the ground were amazed to see this strange sight and began calling out to each other. The foolish tortoise, thrilled to be the centre of attraction, began talking to them but as soon as he opened his mouth and let go of the stick, he fell to his death.

The moral of this tale is: 'One who heeds not words of advice from friends who care about his welfare, meets a sudden end.'

The nullah had its good days and bad, depending on the rains. Sometimes it shrank to a frail line of muddy water with bits of leaves floating in it but on rainy days it became a gurgling stream, attracting a host of bird and insect life. On such days the neighbourhood stray dogs had a great time, jumping in and out of the water and barking with joy as if they had discovered a new playground. One day I saw a cow standing mid-stream, looking deep in thought as she chewed on the fresh green grass. A pair of Little Egrets were keeping her company by sitting on her back. She seemed happy to have the birds scratch her back but was soon taken away by her owner. Despite it being muddy, dirty and narrow, I liked my friendly neighbourhood monsoon nullah as much as Mole from *Wind in the Willows* loved his river. This is how he felt when he came upon his beloved river for the very first time:

> Never in his life had he seen a river before—this sleek, sinuous, full-bodied animal, chasing and chuckling, gripping things with a gurgle and leaving them with a laugh, to fling itself on fresh playmates that shook themselves free, and were caught and held again. All was

> a-shake and a-shiver—glints and gleams and sparkles, rustle and swirl, chatter and bubble. The Mole was bewitched, entranced, fascinated. By the side of the river he trotted as one trots, when very small, by the side of a man who holds one spellbound by exciting stories; and when tired at last, he sat on a bank, while the river still chattered on to him, a babbling procession of the best stories in the world, sent from the heart of the earth to be told to the insatiable sea.

The rainy days seem endless and now we long to see the sun. Clothes smell musty, my dogs smell even worse and all kinds of strange-looking fungi grow in dark corners of the garden. I feel some weird being will suddenly rise out of the primordial, green and brown soup that our lawn has become. Mosquitoes fat with our blood fly around drunkenly as frogs hold noisy political meetings under my window all day. Once in a while, an extra-vocal member of the party gets eaten by a kite hovering above but another frog quickly takes its place on the podium.

Our muddy little nullah gushes on happy in the company of the blue kingfisher, frogs, tadpoles and an odd snake or two and on some days when the rain plays truant, it becomes so quiet that I think it has vanished into the earth.

It was on a quiet, rainless day that the snake, which my mali insists was a cobra, came to visit us. We found it relaxing in a flower-pot, its lethal hood folded neatly and harmlessly like a cowboy's gun resting in its holster when he is drinking in a bar. Everyone in the house raised an alarm but no one knew what to do. My cousin visiting from Kolkata, the family expert on snakes, ghosts and fish curry, remarked it was a baby cobra and said we should leave it alone.

'It will go away on its own,' he said, waving his hand towards the snake recklessly. The snake annoyed by his voice or at being called a juvenile, suddenly rose up. It was no more than a foot long but with its hood flared in rage, it looked very dangerous.

'We should call the police or maybe the fire brigade,' someone said. Our house happened to be almost next door to the fire station though when we had called them once when my old car caught fire, they came with a loud and impressive jangling of bells but shot right past the house. They reversed the huge fire engine but this time they went too far back. By the time they finally managed to come into our driveway the fire had died down.

The snake watched us with lazy, hooded eyes as we watched it anxiously. As we wondered what to do, we voiced our opinion to one another, although nobody actually did anything. Then, the cobra, obviously bored with our hysterical chatter, slowly crawled down from the flower pot and made its way into the shrubs. I did not allow the children to go out into the garden for many days but soon we all forgot about the young cobra as the rainy season brought more (but less dangerous) wildlife into our flooded garden. A mongoose, a vole, a few bats and a family of cats came to seek shelter in the wild green jungle which my garden had become during the rainy season.

This piece by Jim Corbett (from *My India*) about finding a cobra in his bathtub never fails to impress me and I find it more thrilling to read than his many encounters with man-eating tigers:

> I had spent most of that day on the coal platform so did not spare the soap... With lather on my head and face that did credit to the manufacturers, I opened my eyes to replace the soap on the bath mat, (and) to my horror, saw the head of a snake projecting up over the end of the bath-tub and within a few inches of my toes. My movements while soaping my head and splashing the water about had evidently annoyed the snake, a big cobra, for its hood was expanded and its long forked tongue was flicking in and out of its wicked-looking mouth. The right thing for me to have done would have been to keep my hands moving, draw my feet away from the snake slowly and step back towards the door, keeping my eyes on the snake all the time. But what I foolishly did was to grab the sides of the bath and stand up and step backwards, all in one movement. My foot slipped and while trying to regain my balance a stream of water ran off my elbow on the wick of the lamp and extinguished it, plunging the room in pitch darkness. So here I was shut in a small, dark room with one of the most deadly snakes in India.

Corbett spent a long, terrifying hour in the bathroom with

the snake till he was finally rescued by his loyal servant.

On monsoon nights thunder rages away and in the morning the gulmohur leaves, freshly bathed by the rain, sparkle once more, and amongst the foliage our dumpy little Coppersmith pair huddle close together, fat raindrops falling on their jaunty, red-capped heads. The splash of red on the Coppersmith's forehead always reminds me of the gulmohur flowers which have all gone now taking the memories of hot summer days with them. The birds are not so talkative for some reason—perhaps they need the warmth of a hot sun to be able to talk, laugh and tell never-ending stories to each other.

Albizia lebbeck, or the siris tree, has fragrant powder-puff flowers which seem to like the rain and raise their bright yellow faces to the sky happily. The shisham was once a favourite roadside tree and the timber was considered very valuable. It was used to build boats and carts and probably chariots too for kings.

Dove in its nest.

The little Brown Doves coo listlessly as usual in their complaining voice and I always feel this bird, though gentle and mild tempered, is full of self-pity. Their cousins the Collared Doves, have equally meek natures yet both these doves are clever enough to build their nests on the same tree as a Black Drongo. This aggressive and active bird likes to perch on the highest branch of a tree and from here it makes quick, swooping attacks to catch insects. It has a short temper and will often chase a much bigger bird if it feels its territory has been invaded. The Hindi name for this slender, black bird with a forked-tail is kotwal, or policeman, but I think the drongo is much faster, slimmer and more alert than any Delhi cop I have seen.

There are several kinds of drongos seen in our region and each one is a brave fighter, much admired by other birds. The greater Racket-tailed Drongo is the most handsome member of its clan with its crested head and long tail-rackets which float about gracefully as it flies. But this bird does not visit Delhi and prefers the green coastal areas and the bamboo forests in the eastern part of India where it can be heard screeching loudly unlike our strong and silent drongo.

Above the sound of falling rain I can hear the sparrows chatting loudly. There is great excitement of some kind rippling through the entire peepal tree, probably a male sparrow trying to attack another male sparrow who has insulted him or some other sparrow scandal in making. It does not take much to create mayhem in the sparrow family. These little birds are quick to lose their tempers and I have seen them take on crows in a street fight. It is good to see these birds roosting on the peepal since their numbers are swiftly dwindling in Delhi. No one can explain why since sparrows have always lived with us amicably, sharing our homes, our leftover food and participating in every family occasion.

As a child, I remember there were at least three sparrow families nesting on our veranda at one time. My mother was very protective about the birds and we were never allowed to draw the curtains or put the fan on if there was a sparrow in the room. We often waited, sweat pouring down our faces, as the sparrow flew around trying to make up its mind whether to stay indoors or fly out to meet its friends. Visitors to our house were warned not to talk loudly if there were eggs hatching in our resident sparrow's nest or the fledglings were sleeping.

One evening I heard my mother say, 'You have started coming home very late. This will not do. You must behave yourself. The chicks are getting upset and you disturb the others.' My brother and I were surprised at her belligerent tone and quickly went out to see who was being reprimanded. Our father too looked very puzzled. We soon found out to our surprise that she was talking to a male sparrow perched on the fan and the bird looked suitably ashamed though he did not change his wayward ways and continued to disturb the peace of the house.

While the sparrows fluff out their damp feathers and squabble, real menace hovers nearby, unseen by the happy

sparrows or the crows whose lives will soon change forever.

Its glossy head wet and glistening as if combed back with Set Wet gel, the Ruby-eyed koel watches the crow's nest on the peepal tree like a private detective watching a suspect's house. The female, its partner in crime, is lurking on the topmost branch of the tree waiting for her chance. The koel couple has mastered the art of deception; con artists can learn a few tricks from these clever birds. While other birds spend hours building their nests and then put in a lot of effort feeding and protecting their brood, teaching them how to eat with their mouths open, how to fly and how to catch the juiciest worms, our koel couple just know how to have a good time. They fly about singing and chasing each other happily around trees whispering sweet nothings and once in a while they stop as the male picks out ripe berries for his beloved to eat.

When the wooing is over and time comes for the female to lay her egg, the game of deception begins. The koels select a poor, unsuspecting nest owner, usually a babbler or a crow, and then one morning the male koel goes out to deliberately pick a fight. While the crows, the original nest owners, fly out to defend their home, the female koel swiftly moves in and lays a single egg. Sometimes she may lay two eggs if she is in the mood and there is enough time.

Then the koels fly off into the sunset, laughing with glee. The crows return to their nest and carry on with life, totally unaware of what has happened.

This imposter egg hatches before the rightful heirs of the nest and not only does the chick gobble up all the food the foster parents bring home but often pushes out the real babies from the nest like a prince killing its siblings for the throne. Then one day the imposter bird flies away, leaving the unfortunate duped parents shocked and confused. 'Where did we go wrong?' they cry as the young koel begins to sing far away.

Almost the entire cuckoo family is famous for playing this trick but for some reason the birds it dupes have not figured out the deception though it has been going on for thousands of years. You will see crows getting hysterical when they see a koel near their nest but since the poor crows are often agitated no one takes notice of their righteous complaints.

You need a lot of patience to sit and watch birds and study their interesting and odd (only to us) behaviour. You have to learn to stop and stare at a tree to admire the patterns on its bark, its leaf formation, the shape of the flowers and the branches. You have to also learn how to ignore the rude comments of passersby who think you are mad and sometimes you can get into serious trouble for this innocent pastime.

I almost got arrested once while waiting to spot the Golden Oriole. I had always been fortunate enough to catch a fleeting glimpse of its yellow-gold feathers on an old flame of the forest tree that grew outside the Chinese Embassy gate, so I made my way there one day armed with my binoculars. My ten-year-old daughter Shonali was with me and that was what saved me from years in jail. As we stood under the tree, enjoying the cool, rain-scented breeze, I suddenly saw the oriole emerge from the neem tree right next to the gate. I raised my binoculars and tried to focus on its kohl-rimmed eyes but then I felt my daughter tugging at my kurta. I ignored her since the oriole was right above me now, but Shonali began crying and tugged even harder. 'What is it?' I asked, a bit surprised. Then I saw the line of policemen marching towards us. I stood frozen, holding my daughter's hand.

'Madam, what are you doing?' asked a policeman, a senior man judging by his girth.

'Umm...watching birds,' I replied, pointing to the empty branch. The elusive oriole had fled into the safety of the foliage long ago.

'I see no birds. You have to come with us. This is a high

security zone, don't you know? The Chinese minister is arriving tomorrow,' he said, pointing to the high gate beyond which was the citadel of the Chinese Embassy.

I was marched to the waiting police van. The guards at the gate watched me, holding their guns close to their chests, and suddenly I felt I was a heroine in a Second World War movie.

'My mother watches birds all the time,' said my brave daughter in a loud and clear voice. The senior policeman looked down at her and smiled.

'What is this "birdwatching"—a waste of time. You should be doing something useful with your daughter like physical exercise or maths,' he said in a loud voice. All the other policemen nodded. There was a pause and then, as if commanded by the nature goddess, the Golden Oriole flew out of the tree and glided slowly past us, something it never does—its flight is always swift and short.

'There there look!' I cried. My daughter pressed my hand and hissed, 'Calm down, Ma.'

The senior policeman and his juniors had all sighted the beautiful Golden Oriole and were impressed.

'That kind of bird, I have never seen. Very golden,' he said in a soft voice filled with awe and my daughter quickly dragged me away before I could start converting the Delhi police force into birdwatchers.

There is another bird with golden feathers which is much easier to see and admire. Marching up and down a tree trunk is the Golden-backed Woodpecker who likes to pick up grubs by attacking the bark of a tree. Once it has found an old tree with plenty of food hidden in its crannies, this bird will settle down for a long time. It has a strong pointed beak which it uses with skill to hammer away at the bark and its specially designed feet enable it to run up and down the tree trunk quite easily. You will hear its loud hammering long before you see the bird's jaunty red crest or hear its shrill but cheerful call. I am told the new name for this attractive bird is Flame-backed Woodpecker.

There is a smaller woodpecker often hunting in the same area but this poor relative does not have a golden coat and has to be happy with just a black and white speckled one.

The jamun tree, now full of delicious dark purple fruit, is a popular meeting place for many vegetarian birds and one morning I found sixteen birds on it having a feast. The Green Barbet is here calling in its monotonous voice and not eating much. If there is a club for birds then this very odd-looking creature will certainly be called the club bore. The two different kinds of bulbuls are here too feeding in their usual pugnacious way. While the Red-vented Bulbul grabs the best jamuns, its cousin the Red-whiskered Bulbul tries to chase the other birds away and then bursts into a victorious song.

These common birds of Delhi will be found in any park and garden where there are lots of insects and fruits. The Red-vented Bulbul is not wary of us despite the fact it is often caught and sold in bird markets since it is a very popular cage bird and used in bird-fights which still take place regularly in some areas of Delhi. The other birds feasting on the jamun are the usual parakeets, mynas and green pigeons. A lone koel sits on the topmost branch and the other birds keep screeching abuse at it. They all know the koel is planning to play some trick on them. The wicked, handsome creature smiles quietly to himself and shrugs his wings carelessly as if to say, 'Do I care?'

The jamun tree is not just benevolent to birds but to a family of hawkers which is camping below its branches. The children climb up the tree and shake the branches while the parents collect the ripe fruit. Once they have enough, they make small piles of the best, glistening, purple-black fruits, decorate it with flowers and sell it to passersby. The jamun tree is one of the oldest trees mentioned in Indian folklore and legend says that the ancient name for India, Jambudwip, came from the word jamun. Its fruits are sweet and sharp and have many medicinal properties and are considered an effective cure for diabetes.

The rains continue to flood Delhi and you often get stuck in traffic jams behind a line of broken-down cars and buses. But everyone remembers the parched, dry days of just a few weeks ago and is grateful to the skies for flooding the city.

People of ancient India showed their gratitude to the rain gods with special prayers. As Kalidas wrote:

> Eyeing the rainclouds' dark, majestic hue,
> Richer in colour than their own throat's blue,
> With necks upraised to which their tails advance,
> Now in the rains the screaming peacocks dance.

The rainy season with its dramatic sunsets and playful clouds captivated the imagination of miniature painters the most. The season is associated with Lord Krishna in Pahari miniatures. In Sanskrit poetry his dark blue skin is often compared to a gleaming rain cloud.

The opening lines of the *Gita Govinda*, a poem by the great poet Jayadeva, describe the rainy day when Krishna meets Radha for the first time:

> 'The sky is overcast with dark clouds, the woodlands are black with tamala trees. This boy Krishna is afraid of the gloom of the night. O Radha, take him home,' said Nanda.
>
> 'I meditate on him, whose body is the colour of the dark blue cloud, adorned with the rainbow in the sky, whose tresses are embellished with peacock feathers that ripple with a hundred crescents,' sings Radha in praise of Krishna.

Delhi is always unprepared for the monsoon rains and most of the major roads get flooded. Cars get stranded on various corners with drivers peering helplessly at dead engines under raised bonnets. It was during a downpour that I met the couple who came each monsoon to Delhi from Meerut to make a bit of cash.

My car stalled on a rainy morning and I got out in the pouring rain to look for help. A neatly dressed young man came up to me and said, 'Can I help you?'

I pointed to the car. 'It will not start.'

The man opened the bonnet smartly and did something quickly and the engine sprang to life as if by magic. I was suitably grateful and gave the young man a hundred rupees. At first he refused and then very reluctantly took the note and went away. I was touched by the kindness of a stranger which is so rare in a big city and narrated the tale endlessly to everyone.

Exactly a week later I was in another part of the city and when my car died on me again. I again got out muttering angrily at my car, which was a new model, and looked around for help. I was about to call the garage when who do I see but the same man walking towards me. Thrilled, I waved to him. But as soon as he came near and saw me, he turned around and fled. I was surprised by this odd behaviour. Later when I told the man from the garage what had happened he shook his head and laughed.

'You have been made a fool, madam, I am sorry to say,' he said and then, probably feeling sorry for me added, 'Many people in Delhi have been tricked by this man.'

Apparently this mechanic and many others like him come to Delhi during the rains. They spread out in various car parks where they tamper with some mysterious bit of wire under the car. They keep a watch and then follow you on a scooter as you leave, keeping a safe distance. They know exactly when your car will come to a halt. Then they are there to help you for a small fee, reluctantly taken.

I do not know any other person who has been conned thus but have stopped narrating my story since I look quite foolish and people are not at all sympathetic. They were also unsympathetic when my bag with a set of new sketches, clothes and money got stolen from a car park. A smartly dressed man walked up to me as I got out of my car and said, 'Look, you have dropped some money.'

'How kind of you to point it out,' I replied and bent down to pick up the notes wondering how I had so many new notes in my bag. When I turned around my bag had vanished from the car.

Duped once more by the human koel.

The rainy season is not just a time for clever con artists though. It also brings out the peacocks.

The peacock was always closely associated with Krishna in Hindu mythology. Come the rains, and he dances all day long to impress his mates who seem indifferent to his efforts. The hens call in their cat-like voices as they scamper around looking plain and dull in their drab brown feathers. I often think they are jealous of the male's gorgeous plumes, otherwise who could not stop to admire this truly magnificent display. This bird has been painted by folk and miniature painters for hundreds of years and its graceful form can be seen in temple sculpture all over India. Silk sarees, terracotta pots, gold and silver ornaments, wooden furniture and carpets have all been decorated with peacock patterns.

The peacock and the nilgai are considered sacred so no farmer will ever harm them even when they do a lot of damage to young crops in the fields. Nilgais roam around happily munching through the wheat crop and I have seen peacocks living cheek by jowl with villagers in tiny mud huts—they are given food and water along with sleeping space on the roof.

'I do not mind the birds, but what really annoys me is the way the male keeps calling all day in his harsh voice,' said a farmer when I asked him about his resident peacock. 'I do not understand why god has given this beautiful bird such an ugly voice. It is like meeting a beautiful woman and then when she starts talking in a screeching voice, you do not admire her any more. I have seen that happen too. Who can understand the way god's mind works,' he said and went back to watching the peacock dancing in the rain. I wonder what his pretty wife, sitting quietly beside him, sounds like.

The rains do not seem to bother the Coucal or Crow-Pheasant who skulks as usual in the shrubs. I can see it running from one corner of the garden to another, picking up small insects on the way. It has a great fondness for snakes and will quickly grab one in a swift move before the poor thing has a chance to escape. Though it belongs to the cuckoo family, unlike its relatives, it likes to build its own nest and not palm off its eggs on other birds. But it is still not popular amongst other birds since it often steals their eggs for breakfast.

Above the very place where the Coucal is stealthily hunting, there is a noisy, bustling colony of Baya Weavers. These cheerful and energetic sparrow-like birds are experts at building the most complicated nests. You will see these upturned, bottle-like structures hanging from trees, usually tall palms, which are growing near water bodies. The male Baya Weaver, not much to look at just last month, suddenly becomes a smart creature with a bright yellow head and a mysterious black mask. Unlike the male sunbird who sits around preening his new feathers, the Baya Weaver flies around collecting material for his nest.

He usually collects palm leaves or banana leaves and then sits down to methodically tear each leaf he has gathered into long strips. Once he feels he has enough strips he begins to weave them into a neat retort shape with the mouth of the retort pointing downwards to the ground. The Baya Weavers dislike being alone and will always nest in colonies with as many as a dozen neighbours for company. Only the male bird will weave the nest which has a tiny porch and is firmly attached to the branch.

Sometimes the bird will stick tiny mud pellets inside the nest for some unknown reason. Once the nest is finished the male will invite a suitable female bird to visit. This is a very tense moment for the Baya Weaver. Will the female accept his architectural feat or will she not?

She does a thorough inspection and I have once seen her actually pulling at the strands to check if the nest was firmly attached to the palm frond. She looked uncannily like an aunt of mine who used to pull my plaits to check if I had combed my hair properly. I have also seen the female shake her head and go cluck-cluck in disgust when the nest was not to her liking but that may be just a figment of my imagination and not a true fact.

During the inspection, the male sits nearby chewing his nails and then suddenly the female turns all coy. That is a sign that she has accepted his nest and is quite willing to start a family with him. But as soon as she is settled in, the tireless male runs off to build another nest and install another female in it. Sometimes things do not end so happily and the female rejects the nest; then the male Baya Weaver tears down the painstakingly woven wonder. But most of the time the female likes the new home and soon the colony is alive with swinging nests, each with a happy, resident female and her new brood. She is totally safe and secure in her nest since only the weaver birds know how to enter the long tunnel entrance in full flight and no unwelcome visitors can manage to do so.

The insect families have been waiting for the rains too and now they hatch by the hundred. This is exactly what the Bay-backed Shrike has been waiting for. This small, long-tailed, grey, white and rufous bird is the masked-bandit of the bird world. It marks out its territory and then settles down to catch any flying or crawling insect that comes its way. It is an expert hunter and always catches a large amount of flying food. Then, after having eaten a few, it carries the rest of its food away to a safe place which is usually a thorny scrub plant. The shrike looks around with its black eyes to check if anyone is watching and then it quickly impales the worm or insect on the thorn. Now it can come to its larder and eat the stored food any time it likes. This strange but clever habit is how the bird gets its common name of butcher bird.

Delhi has only a few small animals left in pockets of scrub forests, though once it had a healthy population of foxes, leopards, jackals and hyenas. *The Gazetteer of Delhi*, 1912, mentions that:

> The principal wild animals to be found are the antelope (blackbuck), the gazelle (chinkara), pig, hyena, wolf, fox, jackal, hare, monkey and porcupine… Foxes, jackals and hare abound everywhere, affording great sport to anyone with a few dogs.

In fact Delhi's wild life population was a bit too much for the British authorities and the *Gazetteer* says:

> Rewards are paid for the destruction of dangerous animals under the provincial rules: for leopards Rs 5 are given, for male wolves Rs 3 and female wolves Rs 5.

There are no dangerous wolves nor any elegant chinkara to be found in Delhi anymore though I sometimes see a lone jackal on the Ridge. I have yet to see a porcupine though once I found a beautiful needle the animal had left behind in a grassy ditch. I keep it as a good luck charm though it must have been thrown in great anger by the porcupine at an enemy.

When the fields outside Delhi are green with fresh grass and the air gentle and mild after the rains, we decide to go on a picnic to Tughlakabad Fort. The massive structure was built around 1323 AD and the extensive fortifications still look very impressive. Excavations in the 1990s have revealed a secret passage, many complex tunnels and numerous hidden chambers which probably contain remains of long dead enemies.

'There will be snakes,' cry my family. But I want to see the Indian Eagle-owl, an old friend who comes out during the rainy season to hunt for snakes and reptiles. It is a handsome bird with brown and gold feathers which gleam softly in the grey rain-drenched light. *Bubo bubo*—I love its Latin name—is one of the biggest and most powerful owls found in India. It is almost sixty centimetres high and sits firmly on the ground, confident as a mafia don, waiting for some snake, rat or small bird to come by. Unlike other owls and movie stars, it is not afraid of being seen during the day, since it knows it is bigger than other birds. From the ramparts of the old fort, we peer down at it and it looks up at us with a sly twinkle in its big, yellow eyes. Then suddenly there is a ripple and a huge monitor lizard slides past and then another one follows. Our great owl does not even think about picking up this prehistoric looking reptile because it knows it will not taste good. The monitor lizards are said to be harmless but I find them more terrifying than crocodiles. These creatures sit in a pool of mud, perfectly disguised, and move only when forced by hunger or thirst.

The eagle-owl has spotted a small rodent and as we watch, it quickly picks it up and waddles off to a dark corner to eat in peace. After which, it will probably take a short nap.

'What did you bring to eat?' asks my daughter. I bring out some soggy sandwiches, brown bread and cucumber, and my children and their friends groan.

'You always bring such boring things to eat,' they cry.

Suddenly a delicious aroma of pure ghee floats past and we walk ahead mesmerized, following our noses. A family of three is sitting down for lunch and we stand around shamelessly like the freeloaders that we are.

'Please come, have some,' the kind-looking mother says and as I shake my head politely, the children leap forward like savages. Fortunately, the lady has packed enough parathas for an army and we all sit down to eat.

'You must be a school inspector,' says the husband to me and then turns to his wife who is now doling out halva to us. 'I told you, didn't I?' She says nothing.

'As soon as I saw you I knew you were a school inspector and said to my wife, "That lady is a school inspector."'

I hated to disappoint the husband but said I was just watching birds.

'Birds!' he exclaimed in such an angry voice that his

gentle wife put a restraining hand on his arm.

'Have some halva, ji,' she whispered.

The children felt they should offer an explanation since they had eaten so greedily and so well.

'My mother watches birds and she makes notes about them,' my daughter said.

The husband nodded.

'For schools?' he asked hopefully.

I had to step in now to save the situation and said yes sometimes for schools which was not a total lie since I did often take school-children out on birdwatching trips.

'My husband is an engineer with CPWD,' said the gentle wife and the husband smiled at us smugly.

'Today they declared it a rainy day holiday in my office so we have come for a family picnic.' As if on cue five other members of the family emerged from the shadows of the rampart, each carrying a tiffin box.

'This lady is a school bird inspector. She looks at birds, what for we do not know,' announced the husband.

'Never mind, god has made many kinds of people as well as birds and animals. We should live in harmony with everyone however strange they may be,' said the wife kindly and offered us samosas, sweets and hot tea.

'I wish you were a CPWD engineer,' said my children throwing the soggy sandwiches to a group of monkeys. The monkeys turned their backs on us and watched the CPWD family with pure greed. The eagle-owl suddenly gave a low growling call which echoed all over the fort and I eagerly pointed out the magnificent bird to the engineer, hoping to redeem myself in front of my children.

'A bird... No no, it cannot be … looks like a cat to me,' he said, helping himself to a home-made laddoo.

'I know a bird when I see one,' he added, pointing a plump finger towards a crow that had landed near us.

'Recite to madam inspector that English poem about a crow,' he said to his daughter who refused and ran away to play with her friends. But she was dragged back by her mother and made to stand in front of me.

The little girl with an angry look in her eyes began to recite. 'A crow is a black bird. It eats dirty things and does not know how to sing. A crow is not a peacock and we hate crows.' The crow was amused and gave a croak of laughter as it watched the laddoos but we shamelessly ate up ours without sharing any.

As we were leaving the fort an Indian Roller flew down with a flash of brilliant blue feathers, picked up an insect and flew back to the tree. This bird of the open countryside looks very drab and dull when seated but as soon as it flies, you see its lovely colours. If you watch the telegraph wires you will see its brown shape hunched up like an old professor seated at a desk reading his favourite book.

On a grey, cloudy day the Indian Roller's turquoise blue feathers look even more dramatic and you realize why this bird is associated with Lord Shiva who is also known as Neelkanth.

The clouds play in the sky like truant children and very often they do not bring any rain at all. Then the day is miserable with sweat pouring down your skin. It is difficult to go out birdwatching on days like this since I fear I will drop my binoculars in a pool of perspiration like Alice in Wonderland. I sit by the window and hope I will see something fly past. The birds are clever and stay quietly in the shade to conserve their energy. The clouds darken promising rain but then frolic away to one corner of the sky to create strange shapes.

In Kalidas's poem, *Meghduta* or *The Cloud Messenger*, a love-sick hero asks a rain cloud to give his wife a message from him.

> The rains now at hand, seeking to sustain the life
> of his beloved,
> He thought to induce that cloud to carry her news
> of his
> Welfare,
> With fresh kutaja blooms he tendered it the guest
> offering
> And with loving heart spoke affectionate words of
> welcome.

At dusk the sky becomes a sea of brilliant orange-red and not a single cloud can be seen. Fruit-bats fly out silently from the arjun trees of Lutyens' Delhi, hoping they will find some good things to eat tonight.

I can hear crickets calling out to each other in excited voices and far away the owl hoots in eager anticipation of a meal it will soon make of the poor crickets. 'Eat or be eaten' is the rule that all creatures follow in the natural world and it seems to work.

Once I heard jackals calling during the monsoon, on a full-moon night. Their howls had a strange, other-worldly musical quality, almost like heavy metal sounds. 'Must have been the neighbour's dog,' said my disbelieving children.

Not so long ago, Delhi had a huge population of game birds like partridges and quail. I am told by old residents of Delhi that they used to go partridge shooting in what is now Chanakyapuri. 'We would park our car near Teen Murti Lane which was then called Robert's Lane and then walk across into the scrub forest teeming with game birds.'

When my parents built a house in Hauz Khas, my grandmother was alarmed. 'I heard there are tigers there,' she wrote to my mother from Kolkata. She may have imagined it or mistaken a leopard for a tiger.

But she clearly remembered Delhi from the early 1920s when the British ladies used to ride out to hunt jackals in scrub forests around Qutub Minar and refused to believe that Delhi was now a safe city with no wild animals on the prowl except us humans.

Hunting tigers, leopards, game birds and even the poor jackal in the wild was the favourite pastime of Mughal and British rulers of Delhi as well as the maharajas from neighbouring states. Even ordinary people thought shooting ducks and partridges was a good way to pass an idle morning. I remember as a child in 1962, going with my uncles to

Sultanpur Lake for a duck shoot. Fortunately my uncles were hopeless with guns and gave up the shoot after a few fruitless or shall I say 'duckless' rounds and decided to attack the vast quantities of food we had brought with us. I remember the large lonely lake shimmering like a huge silver plate embedded in an empty landscape.

Many other unfortunate animals could not escape the gun and the last three cheetahs in the wild were recklessly shot by the Maharaja of Korea—not the Korea of Samsung and Hyundai but a small princely state in Madhya Pradesh—he thus successfully wiped out the species from India in just a few minutes.

The shikar-crazy Maharaja of Sarguja had the dubious honour of shooting 1,170 tigers in his long, trigger-happy lifetime. Dr Salim Ali, the renowned ornithologist, writes in *The Book of Indian Birds* about a meeting with the maharaja:

> Beaming with joy and self-satisfaction, he announced to me that this was the happiest day of his life because he had shot his eleven hundredth tiger this morning.'

In Keoladeo National Park, Bharatpur, you can see records of massacres of birds by shooting parties. The record for the largest plunder was held by Lord Linlithgow, the Viceroy of India, in 1938, who along with his guests, shot 4,273 birds in one morning. Now hundreds of migratory and resident birds swim around happily in the sunshine knowing they are protected by the Wildlife Protection Act, 1972 and no gun-toting viceroy or maharaja can harm them.

In Delhi, in the green shrubs which the rains have made luxurious, you may find one of the city's few remaining mammals—the wily mongoose. This animal prefers to live near us rather than in the forest and hunts for rats, mice, lizards and frogs mostly after the sun has set and its grey-brown shape can blend into the fading light. It often hunts during the day, too, especially during the monsoon when there are huge numbers of frogs leaping about. The mongoose's long vendetta with snakes has made it a popular creature in folklore and the brave mongoose was made more famous by Kipling in his popular children's story 'Rikki-Tikki-Tavi'.

The fearless mongoose is happy to take on any snake

including the cobra and its chosen strategy is a head-frontal attack which takes the snake by surprise. As the mongoose is extremely agile, it can evade the snake's lethal bite. Many people in the villages believe that the mongoose eats a certain herb called mangus wail to protect itself from snake venom but there is no scientific proof of this as yet.

In ancient India people often kept mongoose as pets so that the house would be safe from not only snakes but rats, mice, scorpions and lizards—all the creatures the mongoose loves to eat. I have seen many mongoose and snake combats in the areas around Mehrauli but these are all paid shows by snake-charmers.

We too have a resident mongoose in our garden which the dogs hate but fortunately for us the mongoose, who is a far superior fighter, is indifferent to their hostility and hunts happily at dusk and dawn, its glossy brown coat rippling like an otter's as it runs after its prey. Once in a while it shows itself to the dogs and gives a teeth-bared, fierce snarl which makes us all tremble with fear.

The rains have made the branches slippery and the squirrels have a tough time running up and down the tree trunk. They like to stay safely in the foliage but sometimes chase each other around the tree and come right down to the ground. This species is called the five-striped palm squirrel to differentiate it from its cousin the three-striped palm squirrel who prefers to live in the forest instead of cheek by jowl with us.

The squirrels have a strange, hysterical, bird-like call

which confuses many of my friends who they insist it is a bird they hear. To make matters more complex, the squirrels live in an untidy nest on a tree and eat only fruits and berries like many birds they share their living space with. A legend from the Ramayana says the squirrels were plain brown creatures till Lord Rama blessed them by stroking their backs because they had helped so tirelessly in building the bridge over the sea to Lanka. Since then, the legend says, they have had these beautiful stripes on their backs.

The clouds gradually move away and the rains are now thinking of leaving too. The days are mild and the sunshine not so harsh or humid. It is still very warm but you can find faint traces of winter in the air. I wake up one morning and look out of the window. The garden is covered in a fine, grey mist and suddenly I feel I am in the hills. The air has a fresh, green scent almost as sharp a pine-scented breeze.

In the hills the rains would have fallen relentlessly making the land so slippery and wet that huge chunks of the hillside would have slid downhill. There, the rainy season is the time the farmer quickly sows the maize crop and once that is done he does not have much to do except swap yarns and drink home-brewed wine.

I once saw two farmers work all day in their field, sowing the maize crop and then when it was dusk, they sat down under a tree to drink. They drank and argued all night, their voices rising loud and clear through the silent mountain village. Apparently at one point the argument got so violent that one drunk pushed the other one down the hillside. He

rolled all the way down into a khud—a rocky hollow. There he lay all night in the rain oblivious of leopards, jackals and snakes lurking around him. His family sent out a search party at dawn and could not find him.

'Must have been dragged away by the leopard,' said his friend, not one bit worried. To my surprise, I found both of them sitting side by side again that evening with their arms around each other and a bottle by their side.

'Drinking partners never fall out,' remarked an old village woman as we watched them singing loudly in the rain.

In Delhi, the thunder no longer rolls and the sky is a clear blue now. The trees are still fresh and green but many of them are slowly changing their colours to greet the brief autumn season. The alstonia scholaris now brings out a few tiny creamy white flowers and their powerful spicy scent fills the air. 'Soon it will be winter,' whispers the tree as it spreads its perfume. One of the Hindi names for this tall handsome tree is shaitan because people in ancient times believed that the Devil lived on this tree and they warned travellers not to sleep in its shade. The logical explanation was that the sweetly scented flowers attracted hordes of insects to the tree. Wherever there is an abundance of insects, birds gather and snakes often come to make a meal of these birds. So in a way it was to keep people safe from snake bite that the alstonia was named shaitan. The English name is derived from the fact that the wood from this fast-growing tree was used to make blackboards for schools. I like the Sanskrit name saptaparni, which describes the seven leaflets which make up its leaf.

Every day, the air gets a little cooler and just when we are lulled into thinking the cool weather is upon us, the day turns hot and humid once more. The monsoon lingers on but it only rains once in every eight or nine days, refreshing the trees and allowing new plants to grow. I look out of my window and I count eight shades of green and then as I am about to turn away, I am surprised by a patch of purple-blue in the sea of green. The jacaranda has decided on the spur of the moment to bring out a small spray of delicate flowers as a farewell gift to the monsoon. The grey light is just right for the delicate blossoms which do not like the sun.

As the clouds gradually float away like huge ships sailing into the horizon, we say farewell to the benevolent rains with these words of the great Sufi mystic and poet Rumi:

> Beware! Don't allow yourself to do
> what you know is wrong, relying on the thought,
> 'Later I will repent and ask God's forgiveness'
> True repentance flashes inside and rains tears.
> Such lightning and clouds are needed.
> Without the lightning of the heart
> and the rain storms of the eyes,
> how shall the fire of Divine wrath be calmed?
> How shall the greenery grow
> and fountains of clear water pour forth?

EPILOGUE

'We think clouds are Nature's poetry, and the most egalitarian of her displays, since everyone can have a fantastic view of them.

Look up, marvel at the ephemeral beauty, and live life with your head in the clouds!'

—From the Manifesto of the Cloud Appreciation Society.

Sparrows bathed in muddy pools; hornbills flew above our cars during traffic jams but we hardly gave them a passing glance. Our days were busy, bustling with chores and endless activities. We went around meeting friends in crowded places; we commuted to our work places, unmindful of the close contact of strangers. We enjoyed travelling to various destinations, with no undue concern except about delayed flights or lost luggage. When I wrote this book in 2014, COVID-19 was a term unheard of. We had no idea that within five years, our lives would be changed forever. The Ides of March struck with a vengeance in 2019 and menacing, dark clouds of sickness and death gradually engulfed us, as every country in the world was impacted by the deadly Corona virus . People, rich or poor, young or old, weak or in the prime of health, succumbed to the deadly virus. Regardless of where they lived, they were traumatized by severe illnesses, developed unheard of disabilities, and had to cope with the tragic loss of many loved ones. This world-wide pandemic created a state of intense panic that was last seen only during the Second World War.

The evening before the lockdown began in Delhi, I fled to my home in Shaya, situated in a remote hilly area of Himachal Pradesh. The next day the state borders were sealed and we became prisoners in Shaya village. I was fortunate enough to have a large orchard to roam around in but my siblings and friends could not leave Delhi and were confined to their homes in the city.

Guilt-ridden, I would talk to my brother and sister every day and every day I heard tales of horror and saw frightening images on television. Panic-stricken people crowding the hospitals, exhausted doctors being overwhelmed by thousands of patients, elderly people gasping for breath, begging for oxygen cylinders.

'Our medicines have finished and the local chemist shop is shut since the owner is in hospital.'

'Our household help cannot come for work and my elderly parents are suffering but I can't go and help them.'

'We haven't got any vegetables or milk for the children for the last five days. I have run out of cooking gas.'

'My doctor cannot see me till next month. I am a cancer patient.'

The COVID nightmare continued as people somehow tried to cope, though life continued to get more and more difficult. In between the dark, gloomy news, there were humane stories of how total strangers helped each other and shared their limited resources. My sister's live-in help, foraged the local park for wild 'saag' and shared it with her. An elderly neighbour's guard walked all the way, almost five kilometres from the outskirts of Delhi, to drop milk and bread at her gate every morning.

During those dark, dismal days, many of my friends and even total strangers got in touch with me, asking me the names of trees and birds they had seen. 'We are locked up at home with our kids. We sit and watch the trees from our windows all day and the children keep asking us the names of the birds. We have no idea since we never had time to just sit and look at birds and trees before.'

'I have just recovered from COVID and am too weak to walk around. I sit in my balcony all day and look at the trees. They soothe my tired eyes.'

'I have planted a few chilli and mustard seeds and the seedlings have sprouted at last. They make me feel happy and for a few minutes I forget my pain.'

'I am a prisoner in my small flat. I watch the clouds from my window and marvel at their fantastic shapes. They help me pass the endless, lonely hours.'

As the horrific days passed in bewilderment and chaos

and people mourned the death of relatives and friends, many of them discovered the healing power of Nature; the soothing sound of birds calling; the quiet green, the healing aura of trees, the gorgeous sight of clouds as they travelled across the sky. Suddenly, all these natural, everyday elements came alive with a new meaning; it seemed very important now to notice them; to listen to what nature was saying to us. All the things we had taken for granted till now, suddenly seemed vital for our well-being, for our mental health and even for our survival.

Suddenly people could hear birdsong at dawn since there was no noise of traffic. The empty roads now belonged to birds and many of them were spotted in unlikely places. 'The parks have turned into jungles. I saw a purple heron the other day in Sunder Nursery,' said Gillian Wright, my bird-watching friend.

My sister called to say that a large white bird was sitting in her balcony. We identified it as the White Egret, commonly seen in farms and paddy fields on the outskirts of Delhi.

My neighbour Aneel Stanley, a keen birdwatcher and an ace bird-photographer, said, 'I saw Golden Orioles and golden flame-backed woodpeckers for the first time in Garden Estate. There are many more sparrows here too.'

Sparrows, now not so commonly seen in Delhi, since the overcrowding in the city has destroyed most of their safe habitats, came out of hiding since there were many more wild seeds to be found on the empty roads along with safe nesting sites in the quiet city. News of rare water birds being sighted in cities came from other parts of the country as the deadly virus carried on unabated.

Depressed by the sad news from Delhi, I began to reread my books on natural history to help calm the anxious thoughts racing through my head. Earlier, I had read these books for pleasure but now I discovered that words written in praise of Nature carried a unique healing power. They comforted me like the companionship of an old, trusted friend.

These lines written by Ruskin Bond, helped me and many others to overcome the fearful and anxious thoughts we were all struggling with those days: 'Is Nature your religion?' someone asked, just the other day. It would be presumptuous to say so. Nature doesn't promise you anything—an after-life, rewards for good behaviour, protection from enemies, wealth, happiness, progeny, all the things that humans desire and pray for. No, Nature does not promise these things. Nature is a reward in itself. It is there, to be appreciated, to be understood, to be lived and loved.

In a poem written almost a hundred years ago by William Waterfield, the poet describes for us the joys of spring in north India:

'The breeze moves slow with thick perfume
From every mango grove;
From coral tree to parrot bloom
The black bees questing rove,
The koel wakes the early dawn.'

As I went through my tattered old bird books, I saw that I had been to Sultanpur Lake in March 1983 and seen 1,500 flamingoes and been stung by a bee. This made me look up bee facts and I learnt that an adult worker bee works very hard from when it is born to the day it passes on and does not just fly from one pretty flower to another, collecting nectar and gossiping with other bees, as is commonly believed. These are its duties from the day it is born:

Day 1-2: Clean cells and keep the brood warm

Day 3-5: Feed older larvae

Day 6-11: Feed younger larvae

Day 12-17: Produce wax, build comb, carry food, ripen honey

Day 18-22: Guard the hive entrance

Day 23 and till it passes on to its next life: Fly from hive to pollinate plants, collect pollen, nectar and water.

So the next time you are stung by a bee, show the tiny creature some respect because it has a tough life!

As the days went by, the trees in the orchard revealed an abundance of new flowers, bees gathered nectar frantically, and the langurs behaved as wildly as they always did. They played havoc all over the orchard, tearing branches and nibbling at the peach and plum blossoms, digging up the vegetable seedlings. The hillsides were covered with wild flowers and fresh, green grass.

Nature seemed unconcerned about the raging pandemic though I am sure she was looking at us humans and shaking her head sadly and whispering, 'Wake up before it is too late!'

As I walked around the orchard, I would often take a leaf in my palm and carefully look at the intricate pattern on its surface. It somehow helped me to feel better. I asked many of my friends to do that. A year earlier, they would have laughed at this suggestion and called me a crazy nature freak but today they listened to me. Maybe a bit reluctantly, but they did listen. The children were the ones who responded at once to my somewhat strange suggestions. 'Wash a few leaves and arrange them according to their shades. Examine each vein. Count the petals on a flower and then draw their shapes, one by one. Count how many ants you have seen today. Follow their travel path. When you wake up, listen to the different sounds of bird calls, before you open your eyes.'

'I did listen but I only heard my father snoring,' said one child. Another one said that she had heard the birds singing away, despite living very close to the metro station.

I have mentioned how you can see magnificent birds like Grey Hornbills when stuck in a traffic jam. Even in the crowded areas of the city, above the din of honking cars, you can hear so many birds calling. You just have to listen very carefully. Take a few minutes out to look at the tree standing so majestically outside your house. There is so much bustle and activity going on there and for a few moments you will become lost in their marvellous world.

As I write this, I can see a few sparrows bathing in a puddle of rain water outside my window. There is a very strict hierarchy in the bird swimming pool. First the parakeets fly in, after they have finished splashing about, the mynahs troop in one by one. By now the pool is really muddy but this is the way the sparrows like it. Fluffing up their feathers, they hop about, chatting to each other all the time. Then they fly to a dry patch on the ground and do a quick dust-bathing spa. This is an essential part of their preening routine since it gets rid of any tiny bugs lurking in their feathers.

Now that we are free from COVID anxiety and can roam around again, people are travelling relentlessly, exploring remote areas, searching for unspoilt places. 'I want a lonely cottage in a dense forest with no neighbours for miles,' said my friend. 'We spent almost two years locked up in a small flat with our three kids. I want to roam free as a bird now. I don't want to hear any human voices.'

Last week I went to the huge, rambling Biodiversity Park in Gurgaon and was amazed at the new variety of trees and shrubs growing there. I knew the names of just a few but I realized that this must have been the original vegetation of the Gurgaon region before it was all built up with glass and concrete buildings.

Yellow and white butterflies chased us and hundreds of munias chatted with each other as they searched for seeds amongst the dry, thorny shrubs. A pair of Purple Sunbirds glided across, the male showing off its iridescent, new plumage. The air carried a faint scent of keekar blossoms. Suddenly, we saw a mongoose run across, its sleek glossy brown body merging with the dry earth. A few smart young boys posed for selfies, leaning against an old neem tree, and were rewarded at once by sharp bites from an army of ferocious red ants.

The endless, lonely COVID days made us all realize the healing power of Nature once again but it should not be that we seek Nature's healing touch only when times are bad. Look at her; touch and listen to her each and every day of your life. Wonder at the grand and also the tiniest things she gifts us; marvel at the magic you become a part of, as the earth renews itself over and over again, regardless of how we treat her. Increasing noise and air pollution is creating havoc with the birdlife in the city. We need to create safe habitats for them by planting more trees and rewilding many more areas in the city, which will allow bird and insect to flourish. We cannot go on with this mindless 'beautification' of Delhi's beautiful old parks, which destroys safe habitats.

We will all disappear into the ethereal world one day but Nature, an intrinsic part of our being, is forever.

SOURCES

Wind in the Willows by Kenneth Grahame; Methuen and Co Ltd, 1951

The Jungle Book by Rudyard Kipling; MacMillan and Co., 1957

Gita Govinda by Jayadeva

Kumarasambhava by Kalidas; Sahitya Akademi

Alice in Wonderland by Lewis Carroll; Hamlyn Publishing, 1965

My India by Jim Corbett; Oxford University Press, 1991

British Social Life in India by Dennis Kincaid; Routledge, 1938

Poems from the Sanskrit Translated by John Brough; Penguin Books

Up The Country by Emily Eden; Richard Bentley, 1866

Gitanjali by Rabindranath Tagore; Sahitya Akademi

Meghduta by Kalidas; Sahitya Akademi

The Book of Indian Birds by Salim Ali;The Bombay Natural History Society, 1941 Poems of Rumi

Ritusamhara by Kalidas; Sahitya Akademi

APPENDIX

List of birds and plants that appear in the book

Winter

BIRDS

Bar-headed Goose *Anser indicus*
Blossom-headed Parakeet *Psittacula roseata*
Bluethroat *Luscinia svecica*
Bronze-winged Jacana *Metopidius indicus*
Chukor *Alectoris chukar*
Collared Scops Owl *Otus bakkamoena*
Common Crane *Grus grus*
Common Sandpiper *Tringa hypoleucos*
Common Teal *Anas crecca*
Common Quail *Coturnix coturnix*
Coot *Fulica atra*
Dalmatian Pelican *Pelecanus crispus*
Darter *Anhinga rufa*
Demoiselle Crane *Anthropoides virgo*
Flamingo *Phoenicopterus ruber*
Gadwall *Anas strepera*
Grey Partridge *Francolinus pondicerianus*

Greylag Goose *Anser anser*
Himalayan Quail *Ophrysia superciliosa*
Indian Moorhen *Gallinula chloropus*
Indian Nightjar *Caprimullgus asiaticus*
Little Cormorant *Phalacrocorax niger*
Little Egret *Egretta garzetta*
Little Stint *Calidris minutus*
Lorikeet *Loriculus vernalis*
Mallard *Anas platyrhynchos*
Marsh Harrier *Circus aeruginosus*
Pink-headed Duck *Rhodonessa caryophyllacea*
Pintail Duck *Anas acuta*
Purple Moorhen *Porphyrio porphyria*
Purple Sunbird *Nectarinia asiatica*
Red-crested Pochard *Netta rufina*
Ruddy Sheldrake *Tadorna ferruginea*
Sarus Crane *Grus Antigone*
Shoveller *Anas clypeata*
Siberian Crane *Grus leucogeranus*
Spotbill Duck *Anas poecilorhyncha*
Tailorbird *Orthotomus sutorius*
White Ibis *Threskiornis melanocephalus*
White Pelican *Pelecanus onocrotalus*
Wigeon *Anas penelope*
Wood Sandpiper *Tringa glareola*

ANIMALS

Nilgai *Boselaphus tragocamelus*

Spring

BIRDS

Alexandrine Parakeet *Psittacula eupatria*
Ashy Prinia *Prinia socialis*

Black Redstart *Phoenicurus ochruros*
Coucal *Centropus sinensis*
Flame-backed Woodpecker *Dinopium javanense*
Golden Oriole *Oriolus oriolus*
Green Bee-eater *Merops orientalis*
Green Pigeon *Treron phoenicoptera*
Jungle Babbler *Turdoides striata*
Large Grey Babbler *Turdoides malconi*
Large Pied Wagtail *Motacilla maderaspatensis*
Paradise Flycatcher *Terpsiphone paradisi*
Plumheaded Parakeet *Psittacula cyanocephala*
Red-vented Bulbul *Pycnonotus cafer*
Rose-ringed Parakeet *Psittacula krameri*
Rosy Starling *Pastor roseus*
Scarlet Minivet *Pericrocotus flammeus*
Spotted Owlet *Athene brama*
White-throated Kingfisher *Halcyon smyrnensis*
Wood Pigeon *Columba palumbus*
Yellow Wagtail *Motacilla flava*

TREES
Ashok *Polyalthia longifolia*
Coral Tree *Erythrina indica*
Flame of the Forest *Butea monosperma*
Jacaranda *Jacaranda mimosifolia*
Kachnar *Bauhinia variegata*
Peepal *Ficus religiosa*
Silk-cotton *Bombax malabaricum*
Tamarind tree *Tamarindus indica*
Tulsi *Ocimum tenuiflorum*

Summer

BIRDs

Blue-throated Barbet *Megalaima asiatica*
Brainfever Bird *Cuculus varius*
Coppersmith *Megalaima haemacephala*
Great Himalayan Barbet *Megalaima virens*
Green Barbet *Megalaima zeylanica*
Grey-headed Flycatcher *Culicicapa ceylonensis*
Grey Hornbill *Tockus birostris*
Green-backed Tit *Paros monticolus*
Himalayan Tree Creeper *Certhia himalayana*
Koel *Eudynamys scolopacea*
Magpie Robin *Copsychus saularis*
Nuthatch *Sitta frontalis*
Pied-Crested Cuckoo *Clamator jacobinus*
Red-billed Blue Magpie *Urocissa erythrorhyncha*
Red-billed Leiothrix *Leiothrix lutea*
Red-headed Tit *Aegithaliscus concinnus*
Scarlet Minivet *Pericrocotus speciosus*
Whistling Thrush *Myiophoneus caeruleus*

TREES

Banyan *Ficus benghalensis*
Blue pine *Pinus excelsa*
Chir pine *Pinus longifolia*
Deodar *Cedrus deodara*
Gulmohur *Delonix regia*
Indian Laburnum *Cassia fistula*
Mango *Mangifera indica*
Pride of India/Queen's Flower *Lagerstroemia speciosa*
Silver fir *Picea Pindrow*
Spruce fir *Picea Smithiana*

Monsoon

BIRDS

Baya Weaver *Ploceus philippinus*
Bay-backed Shrike *Lanius vittatus*
Black Drongo *Dicrurus macrocercus*
Black-winged Stilt *Himantopus himantopus*
Common Kingfisher *Alcedo atthis*
Greater Racket-tailed Drongo *Dicrurus paradiseus*
Golden-backed Woodpecker *Dinopium benghalense*
Indian Eagle-owl *Bubo bubo*
Indian Roller *Coracias benghalensis*
Peacock *Pavo cristatus*
Red-whiskered Bulbul *P.jocosus*
White-breasted Kingfisher *Halcyon smyrnensis*
White-eye *Zosterops palpebrosus*

ANIMAL

Jackal *Canis aureus*

TREES

Arjun *Terminalia arjuna*
Jamun *Eugenia jambolana*
Shisham *Dalbergia sissoo*
Siris *Albizia lebbeck*